The Panchen Lama's Debate Between Wisdom and the Reifying Habit by PANCHEN LOBSANG CHÖKYI GYALTSEN

The Panchen Lama's Debate Between Wisdom and the Reifying Habit

by

PANCHEN LOBSANG CHÖKYI GYALTSEN

Translated by

KENNETH LIBERMAN

MOTILAL BANARSIDASS PUBLISHERS
PRIVATE LIMITED • DELHI

First Edition: Delhi, ***2014***

ISBN: 978-81-208-3951-9

MOTILAL BANARSIDASS
41 U.A. Bungalow Road, Jawahar Nagar, Delhi 110 007
8 Mahalaxmi Chamber, 22 Bhulabhai Desai Road, Mumbai 400 026
203 Royapettah High Road, Mylapore, Chennai 600 004
236, 9th Main III Block, Jayanagar, Bengaluru 560 011
Sanas Plaza, 1302 Baji Rao Road, Pune 411 002
8 Camac Street, Kolkata 700 017
Ashok Rajpath, Patna 800 004
Chowk, Varanasi 221 001

MLBD Cataloging-in-Publication Data
The Panchen Lama's Debate Between Wisdom and the Reifying Habit by Panchen Lobsang Chökyi Gyaltsen. Translated by Kenneth Liberman
Includes bibliography and index
ISBN : 978-81-208-3951-9
I. Panchen Lama II. Debate III. Wisdom IV. Reifying Habit
V. Gyaltsen, Panchen Lobsang Chökyi VI. Liberman, Kenneth

Printed in India

by RP Jain at NAB Printing Unit,
A-44, Naraina Industrial Area, Phase I, New Delhi–110028
and published by JP Jain for Motilal Banarsidass Publishers (P) Ltd,
41 U.A. Bungalow Road, Jawahar Nagar, Delhi-110007

Contents

Acknowledgements

This translation is the result of the spontaneous and unwitting partnership of five extraordinary Sera Monastery lamas, whose keen interest in this text operated separately from each other. I wish to express my gratitude to Sera Je Khensur Lobsang Tsering, Sera Me Kensur Lobsang Tharchin, Geshe Ngawang Dhargyey, Choden Rinpoche, and Lama Zopa Rinpoche, who contributed their enthusiasm and their ideas to this text, permitting me to bring this translation to fruition.

The principal explanation of this text that I received was generously offered to me by Khensur Lobsang Tsering while he was still Sera Je's Abbot, in 1990. Khensur Rinpoche's commentary provided the basis for the first draft of this translation. His willingness to explain difficult passages was a profound instruction in patience. There are some teachers who will explain a matter happily twice, and other, better teachers who are willing to give an explanation three times without forfeiting a pleasant disposition. Khensur Lobsang Tsering could explain a matter a fourth or a fifth time cheerfully, without losing his sincerity or his eagerness to teach. This by itself was a source of inspiration to me. This was made apparent to me again during my close review of the audio record of the commentary that Khensur Rinpoche gave me prior to completing the final draft of the translation, during which I had an opportunity to make a micro-study of Khensur Rinpoche's kindness in its specific details. It is not possible that I will ever become capable of demonstrating that much patience or kindness to my own students, and this above all else merits acknowledgement.

Sera Je Abbot Lobsang Tsering and Kenneth Liberman

The original idea for this translation came from one of my earliest Tibetan teachers, Geshe Ngawang Dhargyey, the head teacher at the Library of Tibetan Works and Archives in Dharamsala, India, who strongly believed that the Panchen Lama's text was eminently suitable for an

American audience and that it was destined to take a place in world literature. This suggestion was made when I was barely able to read Tibetan phonetics, and I stored the idea away for longer than a decade before commencing the project. I am also very grateful to Khensur Lobsang Tharchin, who was Abbot of Sera Me while I was living at Sera Je in 1991-92, and with whom I visited there, and also to his students Art Engle and Michael Roach who unselfishly helped me secure a copy of the MP-3 audio files of his extensive teachings on this text, given in New Jersey at intervals during the period 1986-1989.

Thanks are also due to the Vajrapani Institute of California, founded by Lama Thubten Yeshe (also of Sera), for allowing me to copy a complete set of the audio tapes of a week-long teaching on this text by another Sera lama, Choden Rinpoche, which were given in Boulder Creek, California, in 2000. While Choden Rinpoche presented the text in a week-long retreat, limiting the time he had for detailed exegeses, his commentary clarified a number of points in the translation that I had been unable to resolve. Also useful were some lexical choices offered by those who tried to translate Choden Rinpoche's fast-moving exegesis of this text. Occasional explanations, amendments and translations interjected by Lama Thubten Zopa Rinpoche (also of Sera) during that teaching, captured the pith of a number of ironies and highlighted vital matters that resided inside the text's words but that might otherwise have been overlooked. Lama Zopa also offered me needed encouragement for this project when it had gotten bogged down mid-way, after I had a couple of major heart surgeries.

Finally, I wish to thank Sera Je *ge tsul* Thupten Gyaltsen, whose motivation, intellect, youthful energy (including his eagerness to learn each new English term) demonstrates that the Tibetan dharma is destined to endure at least through this next generation. His explanation of Shigatse lama Lobsang Jinpa's ninety page commentary to this text, *Relinquishing the Extreme Views That Belong to Reification*, his translation suggestions offered generously at Sera Je during 2012, and our discussion of several difficult passages with antiquated terms and references whose intransigence to my decipherment had endured for two decades, helped greatly to improve the accuracy of this translation. Rereading the entire completed translation closely along

The assembled monks of Sera Je Monastic University, Bylakuppe, India

with the Lobsang Jinpa commentary afforded me the additional opportunity to catch scattered translation errors that were lurking inside the manuscript. In this regard, special thanks are again due Art Engle for making me aware of the commentary and for providing me a photocopy of it.

I wish to express my gratitude to the American Institute of Indian Studies whose Senior Research Fellowship sponsored part of the work on this text. The American Institute of Indian Studies also twice provided valuable assistance in securing the Protected Area Permit from the Government of India that is required for any Westerner who wishes to live with Tibetans in the Bylakuppe settlement of South India. Special thanks are due the AIIS Director Purnima Mehta for her excellent efforts in this regard.

Also I wish to express my thanks to the Sera Je Monastic University administration, which generously provided me with a quiet room in their guest house free of charge in the summer of 2012, where I was able to complete the translation, and also to the Fonds Elisabet de Boer of the Section de Langues et Civilisations Orientales of the University of Lausanne, Switzerland, which sponsored the air transportation between California and Bangalore that enabled me to visit Sera at that time.

The length of years that this effort has required is certain evidence that I am one student of dharma who has chosen to take "the three countless eons path" to attaining liberation. May Lobsang Chögyi Gyaltsen's brilliant insights help make the reader's path more swift.

Introduction

The Panchen Lama's Debate Between Wisdom and the Reifying Habit[1] is a text that was begging to be translated. Not only does it convey most of the principal aspects of Tibetan Buddhist epistemology in a concise and even pithy form, it reformats philosophy as a dramatic play—a spirited conversation between wisdom (*shes rab*) and reifying egoistic habits (*bdag 'dzin*)—which makes its philosophical content highly palatable for the general reader. An artistic *tour du force* as much as a philosophical work, the book is poised to occupy a place in world literature, despite its having slumbered for more than three centuries in a few dozen Tibetan monastic libraries.

Some works invite being translated more than others do, and their content is not the only factor in this. What is vital is whether it is likely that the content will be heard, understood, and appreciated by readers of the host language. Especially with a culture like the Tibetans, who have lived remotely from Europe in space, time, and consciousness, not every text can be made intelligible to Europeans, and some may not be capable of attracting a readership.

Walter Benjamin (1997: 4-5) has observed that translations are more than transmissions of a message, and he has considered of the "translatability" of a text:

> Translation is properly essential to certain works: this does not mean that their translation is essential for themselves, but rather that a specific significance inherent in the original texts expresses itself in their translatability. ... In the case of the most significant works, which never find their chosen translators in the era in which they are produced, their translation indicates that they have reached the stage of their continuing life.

The Debate Between Wisdom and the Reifying Habit was shaped perfectly for translation into English, and it is my hope is that this translation will contribute to the text gaining a continuing life.

The first person to make the observation to me that this text was ideal for translation into English was one of my earliest Tibetan teachers, Geshe Ngawang Dhargyey of the Library of Tibetan Works and Archives, who in the early 1980s suggested that this book was especially fit for an American audience. Because it is a witty intellectual contest filled with satire, derision and irony, Geshe-la insisted that American readers would find it engaging. The certainty with which he voiced this opinion led me to seek out the text, and to consider its translation. It was nearly a decade later that the Abbot of Sera Je monastery, himself from Tashi Lhunpo, the home monastery of the author of the text, offered to teach me the text in a classical "pe-tri" (*dpe skrid*; guidance line-by-line) if I was really serious about translating it into English.

One must proceed with caution here, because it is the legacy of orientalism that the heart of Buddhist philosophical culture is thought to be capable of being transmitted by means of its texts. Written texts are only part of the story, and scholarship that never strays from working with docile texts is fated to never really encounter, or even come to understand, Tibetan philosophical culture.[2] What is important is not the texts but what the Tibetans *do* with texts. One needs to at least witness, if not experience for oneself, the live dialectics of a Tibetan monastic university in order to discover how the ideas found in their texts are used by them to discipline their minds and their reasoning. It is not simply the benefits of formal analytic rigor that the Tibetans learn in the "chu-ra" (*chos rva*), their debating courtyards. They also learn the limits of what formal analysis is capable of accomplishing and some details about how one's own thinking, even logical thinking, continuously deludes itself. They learn how formal analysis can open their minds to new understanding but at the same time can confine their thinking within a prison of reason that scholars build for themselves. That is, not only do they learn in the debating courtyards the significance of the ideas they have read, they learn by means of the negative dialectics that is practiced there how to deconstruct the rigid forms of thinking that *any* philosophical practice must set up for thinkers and that necessarily constrains reflection. One cannot judge Tibetan philosophical culture by their texts alone: one has to witness what they do in practice.

That is where the Panchen Lama Lobsang Chögyi Gyaltsen's text makes a singular contribution by transporting the intense philosophical dialogue of the debate courtyard into a literary form. *The Debate Between Wisdom and the Reifying Habit* displays and employs the same dialectical strategies that Tibetan scholars use to force each other's thinking into corners of thought that neither of two debating scholars has anticipated. Briefly put, with this text the Tibetan "chu-ra" enters literature.

The consequences that result from extended threads of argumentation, in the serial and dichotomous fashion that was first established by Nāgārjuna, are followed up in this text by each debater working collaboratively with each other's ideas. In this way the reader is exposed to what Tibetan philosophical culture *does* with ideas and is not left simply to consider those theses abstracted from the debates that gave them birth. This is a central dimension of Tibetan philosophical life, to which to some Western scholars have been blind.

The Panchen Lama and the uniqueness of his text

Lobsang Chögyi Gyaltsen (*blo zang chos kyi rgyal mtsan*, 1567-1662) was the first person to be a Panchen Lama, who in Tibetan society is second in stature only to the Dalai Lama. He became the Fourth Panchen Lama for the reason that his lineage was retrospectively established all the way back to the Gelug sect founder Tsong Khapa's principal disciple Khedrup Je, who retroactively became the original personage of the Panchen lineage. The

Panchen Lama plays a unique role in Tibetan society, being both a religious and a temporal leader. Responsible for confirming the selection of the incarnations of the Dalai Lama, just as the Dalai Lamas confirm the selection of the Panchen Lamas, the Panchen Lama remains a political instrument even today, as witnessed by the contestation between the Peoples' Republic of China and the Tibetan Government-in-exile over the selection of the present 11th Panchen Lama.

Lobsang Chögyi Gyaltsen is better known for his soteriological compositions than he is for his writing on epistemology. He is the author of the most important prayer recited by Gelug monks, the *Lama Chöpa* prayer, a ninety minute-long series of songs of praise to all the teachers of the Buddhist lineage, a composition of great poetic beauty that is recited twice each month by the assembled monks and nuns of all Gelug orders, including the Western ones. It features a summary of Mahayana philosophy, ethics, and *tantra*, and it incorporates some lively visualizations, such as hundreds of goddesses that fly about while one sings to them using operatic flourishes. The Panchen Lama is also well known for his writing on Mahāmudrā, a form of reflection upon the nature of experience that endeavors to transcend dualism. The present text is less well known, and few Tibetans outside of the Gelug order are familiar with it.

While the thrust of the present work is epistemological, most indigenous Asian philosophy remains oriented primarily to the practical tasks that are entailed when trying to become a better human being. For this reason, research in comparative philosophy is on extremely weak ground if it attempts to reduce Buddhist thinking to philosophical ideas that can be compared with European notions of similar stripes. Although European philosophers, Tibetologists included, are not disinterested in becoming better human beings, they are at least formally value-free and may view reversion to spiritual matters with suspicion. For the Tibetans, philosophical inquiries exist primarily for the purpose of assisting spiritual evolution, making the context of their philosophical reflection something that may not be comparable. Of course, there is a range of thinkers in the Tibetan tradition, with some who are inclined to restrict themselves to formal analysis more than others, but part of what makes the present text unique is how the epistemological matters are seamlessly integrated with the soteriological and even tantric elements of Tibetan Buddhism. One receives the entire picture of Tibetan Buddhism, as it were.

In Tibetan literature it is common to keep topics and texts that are *sutra* in nature (meaning that they refer to the exoteric instructions of the Buddha), separate from the topics and texts that are about *tantra* (which includes meditative traditions and esoteric practices that employ elaborate mental visualization, including the effective use of sexual energy for the purpose of achieving spiritual evolution). Here the topics of *sutra* and the topics of *tantra* are integrated, another aspect that makes this text unique. Even texts that are strictly *sutra* in scope still feature an emphasis upon what the Tibetans call *nyams len*, which can be defined as the cultivation of genuine experiences of insight again and again, so that they become natural to one and so that they can be made part of one's behavior as a matter of habit. A shorter way to define *nyams len* would be "practice," and for Tibetans, the most important words in the previous sentence are "again and again."

One can reflect philosophically or one can meditate, but that does not make either of them "practice." It is "practice" only when it is effective at making one a better human being. Practice—in the sense of cultivating experiences of insight and thoroughly lodging the best philosophical and spiritual insights inside of the mundane routine practices of one's everyday life—is the objective of all the epistemological study that Tibetans undertake. Any text by the Panchen Lama is an ideal place to appreciate this aspect of Tibetan philosophical culture.

What most distinguishes the Gelug sect among the Tibetan Buddhist traditions is its added emphasis upon scholarship and formal analytic reason, and this too is a key feature of *The Debate.* Since one's suffering can be traced back to the ignorant notions in which one has invested oneself, it is necessary to subject one's thinking to thoroughgoing critical analysis. Because one is regularly brainwashed by one's *own* false thinking, this analysis must be quite extensive and sustained over a long period of time, and in this way philosophical reflection becomes a necessary part of one's spiritual practice. As Panchen Lobsang Chögyi Gyaltsen writes, "Formal analysis is capable of guiding one to a very steady realization."

The other sects of Tibetan Buddhism are not hesitant to criticize Gelug practitioners for engaging in too much philosophical analysis. They quite rightly identify how formal analysis can become a distraction to taming the mind and become one more source of egotism. Some of these sects recommend more meditation as a way to silence the disturbing aspects of intellection; however, the Gelug reply that prior to having clarified precisely what the view of emptiness is it is useless to enter into lengthy meditative states of consciousness. The Panchen Lama acknowledges the reality of the problem raised by critics of the Gelug system, but he is unwilling to surrender the priority that he believes formal analytic reflection merits. Instead, he views the task to be to learn how, and when, to use formal analytic reason:

> If one does not know just when to apply reasoning and just when to abide in a stabilized realization of what one has analyzed, then all of these investigations will only cause your head to spin. Too much analysis can become excessive and create one more defective practice; however, not applying reason at all is an even greater flaw. One needs to become very skilled at knowing when to apply formal analysis and when to cease applying it, and one must develop an exceptional aptitude for using reason in apposite ways.

In one of the most profound lines of this text, Lobsang Chögyi Gyaltsen writes, "While clever scholars understand a great many things, they miss the one!" The Panchen

Lama is a singular feature to consider here because while he is fully aware of the dangers of formal reflection, he insists upon its full employment and offers sophisticated guidance about how to rely upon it, offering in this composition a good part of the catalogue of Buddhist reasoning about the emptiness of inherent essences. This exegesis waxes most eloquent in Chapter 7, when wisdom summarizes the relationship of emptiness to appearances and explains how an understanding of emptiness is able to enhance the practice of compassion. This makes *The Debate* a decent place for beginning to consider the philosophical arguments of Mahayana Buddhism.

The Panchen Lama concisely summarizes the heart of Gelug meditative practice in the last paragraph of Chapter 7, and his paragraph-long account there displays how Buddhism among the Gelugpa places analytic reasoning at its core. Here calm abiding is united with a penetrative insight that has gained its maturity by purposefully using the seven ways of investigating the lack of inherent essences. One cannot escape noticing the close proximity of this account with that of the founder of the Gelug sect, Tsong Khapa, and much of what is presented here is Gelug orthodoxy.

A key feature of the text is its sustained criticism of those who denigrate formal analysis and recommend in its place quietist meditative practices, which offer the reader an opportunity to consider an implicit but articulate Gelug defense against some of the criticisms of the other Tibetan sects. In the voice of the reifying habit, one of the two antagonists of the debate, the Panchen Lama satirizes those who believe that learning to sit without allowing anything at all to enter the mind can be beneficial, and his portraits of such meditative practices are at times laugh-out-loud funny. But these criticisms of quietism come from an exponent of Mahāmudrā! So it is not the censure of an effete intellectual; rather, it comes from one who values highly the role of *tantra* in philosophical practice.

How are tantric meditative absorptions useful to a philosopher? It is because in the philosophical quest for a nondual understanding of experience, one is always running up against the limits of language. The fundamental problems of dualism may be analyzed by formal and rigorous means, but they cannot be resolved there, for the reason that a very deep irony rests at the heart of formal analysis: one cannot formulate the direct experience of emptiness—it is ineffable (*brjod du med pa*), according to the Panchen Lama. It is impossible to describe nondual experience in analytic terms because as soon as one formalizes a genuine insight, its scope is narrowed and a new dualism is established; yet humans are condemned to reasoning. The very tool that one uses for gaining a better perspective, once it is tamed and reified, can become a new structure of thinking that alienates, perhaps as just another slogan. Resolving this dilemma, which always and necessary accompanies reason, is one of the objectives of Buddhist philosophical culture.

In one of the more extraordinary chapters of this text, the Panchen Lama explains how one can develop an intense lucidity (*gsal ngar*) or vast awareness (*rig pa zang thal*) that serves as an authochthonic methodology: "the method is that the apprehending is itself *its own real basis.*" Such awareness is not subject to alienation by conceptual structures of its own devising, and yet it involves knowing and it is always informed by rigorous training in recognizing that phenomena do not have inherent essences. Here the perspectives of *sutra* and *tantra* are again joined, and *tantra* itself is used to guide the meditator to a correct understanding of emptiness. The Panchen Lama writes (p. 126), "Each supporting element is absorbed into what it had been supporting,[3] until nothing is left but the NĀDA which attracts all of the mental focus. The result of the absorption of the visualization of the mandala and the gradual dissolution of the deity and the seed syllable at deity's heart is a vast empty clarity that is the fundamental basis upon which the mind relies."

Here the epistemological inquiries are not kept separate from the *tantra*. One of the Sera lamas whose commentary upon the text I studied was Sera Me Khensur Lobsang Tharchin, who explained, "In our practices, especially in our tantric practices, we have to always stand in the middle between nihilism and eternalism," indicating that for the Tibetans' tantric meditation a philosophical component is central. Further, one's meditative practice is intended to contribute to epistemological understanding. The Panchen Lama includes several pages of detailed commentary upon some subtle aspects of higher tantric visualizations, which readers may find illuminating, although this text is far from being a manual on *tantra*. Yet the way that the philosophical matters are integrated with *tantra* is unusual.

The most unique feature of this text, however, is the vitality of its dramatic narrative structure. By placing the philosophical topics into the mouths of two antagonists who sharply contest each other's thinking, the Panchen Lama has created a text that is able to seize the reader's attention. One recalls some of the dialogue of *Faust*, where a similar struggle between virtue and error takes place. When wisdom castigates the reifying habit, the Panchen Lama simultaneously castigates the reader in a way that makes the criticism less didactic and more bearable. When the one with reifying egoistic habits satirizes lame analytic exercises or mindless meditative indulgences, as he does eloquently in Chapter 9, the Panchen Lama sketches the shape of our own flaws in a manner that will be pertinent to the most intimate practices of many readers. Although the text is a short one, it is incredibly revealing, and the advice it offers is more compelling than the advice of lengthier, more moralistic religious genres.

The text has the form of a philosophical comedy. The Panchen Lama's wit, which at times is laugh-out-loud funny, keeps the reader entertained throughout *The Debate*, which further contributes to sustaining the reader's engagement with the epistemological matters. The debating begins with the one with reifying habits getting a good start, and during three early chapters he presses wisdom closely against the ropes. Arguing that he has always been intimate with the mind, the reifying habit insists that it would be inappropriate for him to abandon the mind; and while he himself has always dwelled in the center of peoples' hearts, providing them with all the material riches they have acquired, wisdom has for the most part been missing-in-action and comes around only long enough to create a bit of discontentment. The tension built up this way is not unlike the tension one finds in an episode of "The Lone Ranger," wherein it begins to look like at last the Lone Ranger is about to meet his end, although one knows that somehow he will find a way to prevail. The difference is that reifying egoism is probably more effective than the Lone Ranger's antagonists, and he sustains his brilliant and humorous argumentation until the end of the text, rendering his attack more durable. It is uncommon to describe a philosophical treatise as a page-turner, but on many occasions *The Debate* is one.

At the same time, the Panchen Lama makes liberal use of the poetic forms of Tibetan discourse. Not only do the lines of the text conform to seven syllables throughout (a frequent element of the better Tibetan texts, and an aspect that is not readily translatable), it relies upon the poetic use of homonyms (another common feature of Tibetan poetics, also not translatable), and a rhythmic repetition of refrains, which lends elegance to the Tibetan. Unfortunately, the latter poetic tool cannot easily be transported to English either, for while repetitive phrasing is considered a sign of refinement in Sanskrit and Tibetan texts, repetition is usually tedious when it is rendered into English. A remaining feature of Tibetan poetics, the use of brilliant imagery, is given ample scope in English, and the Panchen Lama's metaphors are both beautiful and revealing; in fact, the text includes a decent inventory of the best metaphors available in Mahayana Buddhism. Frequently, the metaphors are employed with humor as one or another antagonist uses it effectively against the other, such as when wisdom criticizes how noisy in defense of himself the reifying habit has become, commenting, "All brooks make a great clamor, but the ocean sometimes barely announces itself." Whether from the perspective of its poetics, humor, philosophical content, or insight into meditative practice, *The Debate Between Wisdom and the Reifying Habit* offers even the casual reader a rewarding experience and a splendid introduction to Tibetan philosophical culture.

The Arguments

The abbreviated name for this text is composed from the first quarter of its full title: *bdag 'dzin gshags 'debs.* The two words *gshags 'deb* reference the thrust and parry of a dialectical argument, *gshags* being "thrust," "give," "pose," or "present," and *'deb* being "parry," "rebut," or "reply." Most interestingly, *The Debate* occasionally assumes the form of classical Tibetan debating style, such as when reifying egoism declares wisdom's defeat by announcing "kor soom!" which is the traditional way to declare that one has defeated one's opponent.[4] We can even observe the one with reifying habits overusing this declaration, in just the manner that an unskilled debater in a monastic courtyard might overuse it. All of the Panchen Lama's discussions are couched in the idiom of the typical witty, tight, and even theatrical dialectical contest that is common in Tibetan philosophical culture.

The central matter that these disputes address is that the root of our suffering is the habit we have developed of concretizing the meanings of the objects that we perceive, concretizations or reifications that view these objects as possessing inherent existence. As wisdom puts it, "We reify our identifications of objects and then fixate upon those reifications." Wisdom offers a pertinent example of how attachment to a goddesses' beauty can lead to feelings of a love that is thought to have an independent existence, and to be eternal. As wisdom has it,

> You may become attached to notions that you have concretized as things that have inherent essences, but sometimes they will not fulfill your expectation that their attractiveness is perpetual and unchanging, in the way you have conceived them. For example, when you see a woman to whose form your eyes have become attached, her attractiveness gets concretized and her beauty seems to really exist on its own; however, the permanent, inherent quality of this attachment is proven false as soon as you generate new such attachments, which seem to have similarly permanent, inherent existence.

That is, the compelling quality of the beauty of a girlfriend or boyfriend is something one has devised oneself, as if life is somehow improved by cultivating a compulsive attraction. When this leads to suffering, whether through aging, death, a rival's success, etc., instead of learning about the impermanent nature of the notion we have devised, we attempt to resolve our crisis by finding yet another girlfriend to obsess about.

Wisdom's recommendation is to use reason to analyze the situation: "Thorough inquiry will cause one to awaken from this stupor and to recognize that things that seem to have positive, independent existence do not really exist in the way that they appear." The commentator Lobsang Jinpa (nd: 19) here adds, "If you do not analyze it, it seems to exist; if you do analyze it, it does not exist." For Tibetans, however, the success of a formal analytic practice does not arise from one or two applications; rather, one must build within one's habitual praxis of thinking—or inside one's karmic imprints, as it were—an instinctive ability to recognize the false imputations of inherent, "true" existence as soon as they occur during our conceptual constructions. As the Panchen Lama says, "Sentient beings are always victims of their own habits of thinking." To improve the situation one needs to change those habits. This is accomplished by making a "practice" of formal analytic reasoning.

Buddhist inquiry emphasizes the universality and inevitability of our being mistaken about what we have understood; however, it is difficult to recognize being mistaken when one keeps believing one's own propaganda.[5] Wisdom speaks of reification: "Amidst so much self-delusion, you are also ignorant of your own ignorance." Objectifying the meanings that we have projected upon phenomena, and then concretizing or reifying those objects as existing by themselves in the very ways that we have objectified them is the everyday practice of reification that wisdom here tells us we must work to eliminate. The commentator Lobsang Jinpa (nd: 52) boils wisdom's position down this: "Whatever arises as interconnectedly dependent is explained to be empty of an inherent essence; and designations are applied to that. This is the middle way."

The "middle way" is the path between positivism and nihilism, and much of *The Debate* takes up the one with reifying habits's accusations that wisdom necessarily must fall into one extreme or another. Lobsang Chögyi Gyaltsen brilliantly composes the reifying habit's argument using some classical strategies from the Tibetan debating courtyards. The reifying habit argues that whatever view of "emptiness" a yogi in meditative equipoise comes to, it has to involve some formulation, some idea, some concretization, and that necessarily entails some degree of positivism. Even when the practitioner is cultivating the emptiness of reifications, the practitioner must use some false appearance as a basis, which implies that it has some existence.

When wisdom denies that this is necessary, the one with reifying habits concludes that wisdom must then be practicing a form of nihilism. The reifying habit presses this philosophical challenge through much of the debate, and in chapter 11 wisdom offers a graphic illustration of how something that has been identified can lack inherent existence but still exist: wisdom uses two half-glasses of water that are mixed together, so there is no longer any "half-glass of water" that can be identified anywhere, and yet the water is not non-existent. Wisdom's point is that identities can lack essences without any nihilism being implicated by this.

When wisdom suggests that a logical formulation can occur during the process that leads to a meditative stabilization on emptiness but is not active during the actual realization of emptiness itself, the reifying habit invites wisdom to help search for just where any formulation could be active. In a passage that bears echoes from the debating courtyard, the one with reifying habits examines serially the logical possibilities, including whether this analytic function occurs *before* the meditative realization (in which case it would not be able to contribute at the critical time), *after* it (which simply would render it irrelevant), or during the meditative stabilization (which might disrupt the stabilization). In this fashion not only are some fascinating epistemological matters explored, the reader is invited to travel the kind of formal analytic itinerary that is typical of Tibetan debating, just as if the reader was in the debating courtyard. By constructing his text this way, the Panchen Lama brings philosophy to life.

The Panchen Lama is especially successful at demonstrating that emptiness is *not* an emptiness *in general*—like something that might be floating somewhere up in the sky, available for being made an object of veneration—but must always be an emptiness of something *in particular*. The Panchen Lama writes, "If during the meditative stabilization itself the 'I' has no being at all, who could possibly cultivate the *lack* of inherent being? Are you proposing that there can be an emptiness without having anything that is empty?" Such discussions of emptiness make it unlikely that the reader will reproduce the distortions of the Mahayana doctrine of emptiness that were common during early European efforts to understand Buddhism ("Voidness," "The Absolute," etc.), and which interpreted emptiness to be more evidence of the "nihilism" that they believed was rampant in South Asian culture.[6] The point of emptiness is to remove absolutism, not to reestablish it. The Tibetans are much less predisposed to positivist portraits of a fullness of being than are the philosophers of Europe and the Judeo-Christian-Islamic world; however, this is an extensive topic that cannot be resolved here.[7] The Panchen Lama is meticulous in maintaining a critical vigilance that resists turning the lack of inherent existence into another reified truth habit. He writes critically (p. 146), "Even when they witness the emptiness of reality, they reify that lack of inherent existence as if it was one more truly existing phenomenon."

One of the strengths of Gelug negative dialectics is its vigilance about keeping essentialism from reasserting itself, a vigilance that is a natural aspect of their getting their philosophical insights to work in and as their habits of thinking. One aspect that many Western readers will find singular about this philosophy is how the anti-essentialist perspective is consistently given more authority than the positivist perspective; just viewing this, even at a distance, can be salutary for a thinker who is accustomed to the hegemony that positivist thought enjoys in European philosophy and science.

There are other itineraries of Tibetan reasoning that the Panchen Lama offers the reader, logical itineraries that at times become very technical. One of the main problems for proponents of inherent essences is that they run into the problem that most phenomena are composed of parts (the classical example presented by Candrakīrti is that of the chariot); accordingly, an anti-essentialist poses the question of whether the phenomenon exists inherently as an individual entity or as a plurality of components, i.e., as one or as many. If there truly is inherent existence, then all of the parts that make up an entity must also have inherent essences, but that would conflict with the independence of the self-nature of the entity as a whole as the essence that it is thought to bear. For several pages the Panchen Lama summarizes most of the rebuttals that involve whether the inherent existence would be existence as an individual or as many. The repetitiveness of his dialectics offers a display of the complexity and seeming endlessness of Tibetan formal analysis, which offers a demonstration that itself contributes to reifying habit's argument that logical criticism raises so many complexities that it threatens to hinder meditative equipoise. In this way the narrative itself dramatizes the problem in a way that makes it evident, and humorous, for the reader.

A similarly intricate example of Tibetan dialectics is displayed when wisdom interrogates the reifying habit about just when it is that the fundamental inherence of an entity takes place—is it during the past moment, the present moment, or in the future? The transitory nature of temporality itself proves false the reifying habit's claim that an identity is inherent, permanent and without change. The formal analysis practiced by Tibetans is a variety of negative dialectics, but it is negative dialectics with a formal analytic spin drawn from the Pramāṇa (logical) tradition of Indian formal analytic inquiry. Instead of having this unique Tibetan synthesis described theoretically, the reader has the opportunity to witness it first-hand, displayed much as one would encounter it in the debating courtyards.

Additional examples of Tibetan dialectics include the critical analysis of the relation of cause and effect: a cause is seen to be dependent upon an effect, for without any effect there can be no cause. This is an analysis that precedes by many centuries Hegel's similar dialectical argument, in his *Science of Logic* (Hegel 1969: 151). Lobsang Chögyi Gyaltsen also includes a critical deconstruction of the notion of mineness, according to which the things that we possess (e.g., "my hand," "my pen") seem to bear this "mineness" within them, independently of us. Wisdom argues, "If mineness exists inherently, it would have to be something that exists separately from the 'I'," which is absurd.

Among the most entertaining rebuttals are the ones during which the Panchen Lama, in the voice of the reifying habit, offers us critical assessments of various practices of meditation that are employed by those who seek wisdom. The reifying habit points out the irony of "meditations upon the existence of non-existence," and he satirizes those whose practice involves "'meditation' in name only and consists of little more than some sweet composure with a bit of added pious chanting." He accuses most meditators of not knowing what they are doing, a criticism that rings true, and he asserts that "so far as possible, they abide there in a placement meditation, and they may even mistake their infatuation with their own concepts for a meditation on ultimate being." The reifying habit views it to be practically inevitable that "One will begin to contrive the nature of the meditative stabilization," fabricating some imaginary era of good feelings and mistaking it for the profound "vast awareness." The Panchen Lama is especially articulate during his exploration of the contradiction that even an ultimate view must involve *some* imputation of meaning and thereby be its own downfall: "As soon as the meditative stabilization has some objective content, reification has necessarily been at work."

These criticisms include a hysterical portrait of tantric practitioners who gravely wear their hair "up high like a crown" and lavishly adorn themselves with tantric jewelry like conch-shell earrings, garlands of bones, etc. He is equally comical in his characterizations of ordinary practitioners who take all kinds of vows in order to feel pious "but don't really feel a need for them, and so they do not keep a close guard over them." The result of all these arguments is that by their end wisdom is beginning to look pretty foolish; at one point, the one with the reifying habit teases, "Wisdom, my arguments seem to have taken your breath away! Are you growing so weary of all this that you are finding it difficult to say anything?" Of course, wisdom gives as good as he gets, which makes for an entertaining voyage through the world of Tibetan philosophical reflection.

The Central Thought

Amidst all of these thrusts and parries[8] of Tibetan dialectics, the Panchen Lama raises one of the most important questions in Buddhism—the relation between ultimate truth and the conventional reasoning that can guide one to it. Here we have the Tibetan incarnation of one of the most enduring and fundamental ironies of human reason, which is the inability of reason to get past the biases that are embedded in the very same structures that it is using for interpreting and understanding the world. The Tibetan scholars have meticulously identified how our thinking *necessarily* distorts what it thinks, but it also suggests that it has developed a way to go beyond those limits and be able to witness "just-the-way-it-is" (*de kho na nyid*), or suchness (*de nyid*), which is ultimate reality; nevertheless, the fundamental *irony of attempting to formulate what cannot be formulated* sticks to their efforts, and here the Panchen Lama subjects it to satire of the reifying habit, making this philosophical dilemma come alive for the reader. It is an irony of human life, an irony about the human use of reason, that seems to be practically without redress.[9]

The intractability of this dilemma has led some Buddhist meditative practitioners to distrust philosophical analysis, and a variety of meditations that attempt to suppress conceptualization have been devised. In the course of this debate, Lobsang Chögyi Gyaltsen satirizes these meditative practices harshly, and insists that the fundamental flaw of projecting inherent essences cannot be corrected without thoroughgoing philosophical analyses: "If during the meditative stabilization there is no proper cultivation of an active mode of apprehending things, then despite all of your proud declarations about the wonderful meditations you are having, nothing will be accomplished." As I have mentioned, Tibetan philosophy maintains a practical orientation, and the principal objective for them is to get the job done, i.e., to overcome one's habits of ignorant delusions, and by do so doing become "liberated": here "freedom" (*thar pa*) is freedom from *one's own habits* of mistaken thinking. For this, formal analytic reflection is a necessary recourse: "One must develop for oneself an always active self-understanding that reflexively ascertains and examines each reifying projection in its particular details." This is the practical work that a practitioner faces, and it relies upon a methodology that conjoins philosophical inquiry with personal evolution.

Buddhism is full of techniques for turning the details of everyday life into a path to freedom from one's self-afflicted delusions, and Tibetan yogis train themselves in non-obsessive forms of thinking. In the course of this, Tibetan reflection takes a highly epistemological turn. In his commentary to *The Debate*, Lobsang Jinpa (nd: 20) writes, "The meaning that one establishes for any phenomenon is without even a speck of independent being and is developed only by virtue of the names, notions, and terminology that are projected upon phenomena." Lobsang Chögyi Gyaltsen explains, "In order to appreciate that each and every phenomenon is empty of having an inherent essence of its own, one must also investigate how phenomena that bear names are actually empty of possessing those names themselves as something that is inherent in them."

The problem is that the Tibetans' reflections proceed mostly by means of an armory of illustrations that describe how ignorant illusions are generated, and much like European philosophers they seem unable to get beyond a few brilliant illustrations (e.g., the rope that is thought to be a snake) to undertaking more comprehensive inventories of self-deluded thinking—*in and as their lived course*—in their specific details, details that cannot be imagined or even recollected but must be captured and described *in vivo.*[10] That is, while their exegeses are theoretically sophisticated, they remain general. In seems that at times Lobsang Chögyi Gyaltsen recognizes the problem, such as when he writes, "Although one abides in that awareness, one should not become satisfied with that formal understanding of emptiness but continue to actively exercise one's analytic faculties to expose and remove all of the innate tendencies to reify phenomena. This is the way to employ the benefits of leisure and prosperity meaningfully."

The Tibetans' scholars acknowledge frankly that even their best philosophical analyses cannot be what is ultimate, and they continually defer to the "direct realization" of emptiness as what is superior, an experience that the Panchen Lama makes an attempt to describe: "It witnesses, but it does not fasten to anything it sees; it gazes, without concretizing what it gazes at; it meditates without doing 'meditation'." Any student of Buddhism will recognize this as being the crux of the Buddha's message. One finds a similar passage in the *Heart Sutra*: "There is no ignorance. There is no cessation of ignorance. ... There is no path, no wisdom, no primal awareness, no accomplishment, and no non-accomplishment either. This being the case, Shariputra, because bodhisattvas have no accomplishment, they rely upon the wisdom gone beyond, and their minds are without obscurations."[11] This suggests the possibility that one can develop one's understanding without also developing concretized notions that limit the scope of one's experience: *this* is the wisdom "gone beyond." Further, in a Tibetan debate manual on the higher tantric practice of *gsang ba 'dus pa* (*Guhyasamaja*) intended to be practiced daily (Anonymous nd: 72), one recites, "Since all animate and inanimate phenomena ultimately lack any inherent essence, there is no meditation, no object of meditation, and no meditator. All three have a nature that is empty of having any objectivated notion, any unity of identification, or any underlying motive."

In his oral commentary to *The Debate*, the Sera Je Abbot Lobsang Tsering explained to me, "There are two ways to cognize emptiness: the first employs the method of a "noema," that is, an objectivated meaning that is used to direct the mind to a realization of emptiness; the second type is a mind that realizes emptiness directly." A noema (*don spyi*), which is a term for translation that I have borrowed from phenomenological philosophy, is an objectification that facilitates the holding of a thought and acts as a repository for collecting immanent reflections about a phenomenon. It may be said that Tibetan critical inquiry is frequently addressed to the local historicity of various noema that thinkers use for organizing their understanding, and in doing so the Tibetan scholars expose how one idealized thought or another (e.g., "this mountain" in reference to "that mountain," or the relation of action and actor) has been reified. Tibetan scholars pay special attention to when, and how, these objectivated tools for thinking become highly routinized, becoming "truth habits" (*bden 'dzin*) that operate unnoticed in their mundane life. They also are fully attuned to the risk that "emptiness" itself can be made routine and therefore become a cause for further alienation. As wisdom informs us in this text, "Even the truth lacks a nature of its own."

Perhaps the most successful philosophical practice in which Tibetans engage is not in their textual theorizing but the way that they scrutinize their truth habits live, in the midst of their daily dialectical contests in the debating courtyard, the "chura" (*chos rva*). It may be said that there is *more* philosophy happening in the "chura" than there is in their texts. At last, with *The Debate Between Wisdom and the Reifying Habit* we have a literary form in which the benefits of the Tibetans' live dialectical practices makes a fulsome appearance, providing the reader with many opportunities for coming face-to-face with philosophical dilemmas in the very way that Tibetan scholars regularly face them. When the one with reifying habits poses a compelling argument, such as the one mentioned above when he asks wisdom, "As soon as the meditative stabilization has any objective content, reification has necessarily been at work! Or, if reification is truly absent, how can one engage in cultivating anything at all?" we feel that we ourselves are being put on the spot. Here reifying egoism is emphasizing the necessary role that our objectifications of our thinking *must* play in the course of training ourselves how to cultivate the emptiness that can deconstruct these objectifications. He observes, "If I am really absent, how can one engage in cultivating anything?"

Similarly, the one with reifying habits teases wisdom about the ineffectiveness of his meditations: "From my perspective, it is impossible to differentiate between a meditation upon a mind that has been pacified and a meditation upon nothing whatsoever." At times the reader will feel put on the spot. Or, the reifying habit asks, if a mind has really stopped conceptualizing altogether, "How is one able to discern just where one is and is not being vigilant?" Vigilance requires critical assessment, which requires some dualist reflection. As the reifying habit presses wisdom, wisdom seems to be held by the short hairs: "If you claim that the consciousness that is ascertaining reality exists, then it follows that there is some inherent existence there, so I too must exist. If you claim that nothing at all exists, then you are cultivating nothing that is capable of possessing an antidote for correcting obsessive reifications. For these reasons you continue to be unable to harm me." The longer that these issues are suspended between the two antagonists and unresolved, the more they are brought to life for us.

Method of Translation

Readers may ask themselves the question, "What business does a sociologist have translating a medieval Tibetan text?" Certainly, my colleagues in sociology keep asking me this. The text in question here falls squarely within my professional interests in sociology. As I explained to a young lama at Sera, my principal task as a sociologist has been to identify and describe how one goes from objectivating a notion about an object—a *dmigs pa*—to becoming fixated upon that reified object as something that possesses its own inherent essence, incarnating the very notion that one has objectivated. An object of thought (*dmigs pa*) or a noema (*don spyi*) is not in itself anything bad; in fact, it is necessary in order for us to be able to think. It is when it we fixate upon our reified identification of an object[12] that it becomes something that needs to be eliminated.

Such fixated identities are precisely the sort of thing that is reification's habitual way of apprehending the world, or in the words of Lobsang Jinpa (nd: 12), the commentator to Panchen Lobsang Chögyi Gyaltsen's text, "the object fixated upon by reification's habitual way of apprehending things."

The Panchen Lama himself explains,

> Sentient beings fabricate their reality: they objectify every phenomenon as the basis of meanings they have imputed. They project their conceptualizing upon the world, and then say that those things are established truly that very way in themselves. But all of those things are their own fabrications. Just as one perceives a coil of rope as a snake or mistakes a far off pile of stones for a man or takes for water what is only a mirage, one fixates upon these fabrications as truly existing just in the way that they are immediately perceived.

In everyday life, we need to objectivate our thoughts. This is necessary for us to know what they are, for keeping track of our own and others' thinking, and for communicating with others clearly. The *dmigs pa* is how we accomplish that, and what we do with these objectifications is a sociological topic. It is not necessary for us to believe that what we so objectivate exists *in itself*, just in the way we have fabricated it, although that is what happens in much common sense thinking. That is, we *do* need to think with conceptual objects, but we do not need to reify them as absolutes that exist in themselves.

I have pursued studies of this phenomenon in many fields, including formal philosophical argumentation, the practices of professional coffee tasters, communication in conversations, following sketch maps to destinations, etc.,[13] always with an eye for identifying the just-how and just-what[14] of how people construct and believe their own propaganda. *The Panchen Lama's Debate Between Wisdom and the Reifying Habit* offers an eloquent explanation of this area of philosophical-cum-sociological interest, which helped motivate my decision to translate it, once Geshe Ngawang Dhargyey had brought the text to my attention along with his recommendation that it was highly suitable for an American audience.

In 1979, during a visit I made to the monastery of H.H. 16th Gyalwa Karmapa in Rumtek, Sikkim, Thrangu Rinpoche ridiculed the notion I had at the time that I could simply sit and translate great Tibetan texts into English by myself. He said that without the close guidance of a knowledgeable teacher, I would be incapable of understanding enough to undertake any translation. He was most certainly correct. Happily, in this case my translation was guided not by one but by *three* word-by-word oral commentaries (*dpe 'krid*). The first and most extensive was provided enthusiastically by the Abbot of Sera Je, Lobsang Tsering, a great scholar whose original monastery was Tashi Lhunpo, the residence of the Panchen lamas. Khen Lobsang Tsering was very eager to see *The Debate* appear in an English translation, and he was true to the etymology of "painstaking" during his five month-long exegesis of the text, in 1990.

I began the first draft of this translation in the mid-1990s, but a combination of professional responsibilities and heart disease, including two major heart surgeries, kept causing the translating work to be deferred; however, one benefit of the delays was that I was able to secure recordings of two additional word-by-word oral commentaries by Sera lamas, one by Khensur Lobsang Tharchin, who was Abbot of Sera Me while I was living at Sera; and the other by a senior teacher and great yogi of Sera Je, Choden Rinpoche. All three commentaries were digitized, so that the explanations for each line of the text could be swiftly relocated and compared with each other. This translation has benefitted by my being able to consult the detailed explanations of these highly esteemed lamas before a final version was determined. Interestingly, the three commentaries conflicted with each other at a number of the more difficult passages, making it necessary for me to sleuth out the best combination of interpretations. Sometimes I would defer to agreement by two of the three commentators. On a few occasions, when all three interpretations varied, I had to select only one as a basis. There were even a few occasions when I rejected all three interpretations, in favor of the interpretation offered by the mid-19th century commentary by Lobsang Jinpa.

In addition to these three oral commentaries, a number of insightful remarks by Lama Zopa Rinpoche made during the course of Choden Rinpoche's discourses were incorporated into the translation. Given that the original suggestion about translating this text came from Geshe Ngawang Dhargyey, and that my own teacher was Lama Thubten Yeshe—both of them Sera lamas, making six Sera lamas in all—this translation is really a contribution to world literature of Sera Monastery. By using each of the digitized commentaries in a systematic and meticulous way, and by carefully reading and consulting the written commentary (circa 1850) of Lobsang Jinpa, I believe that the translated product is accurate; nevertheless, any competent reader will be able to locate oversights and errors that I have contributed myself.

There may be some controversy over how I have chosen to translate one of the two principal antagonists of *The Debate*: *bdag 'dzin*. After years of struggling with this problem,[15] I settled upon "the one with reifying habits," or simply, "the reifying habit." One element of choosing to translate *bdag 'dzin* this way that works in my favor is that all of the available alternatives ("self-grasping," "ignorance," "egoism," "common sense," "reification," etc.) are more problematic than is my choice. It was while reading through Lobsang Jinpa's commentary that I became very confident about my decision. As Lobsang Jinpa (nd: 25) writes, "The innate habit of reification is to be opposed by cultivating the lack of inherent identity." What is being referenced by *bdag 'dzin* is a specific habit, an activity of consciousness, and not some general state of affairs, like ignorance. It may amount to ignorance, but what matters most are the specific practices of the mind, and "the one with reifying egoistic habits" more closely references those activities; *bdag 'dzin* is closer to being a verb than to a noun. Moreover, it is not what one does not know that makes one ignorant: it is what one *does* know. Our practices of thinking fill up our minds with distortions, leaving no room for learning anything new. As the Panchen Lama says, people are "distracted by being stuck within the ruts of their own bewildered thinking." "The reifying habit" better references those practices and ruts. Egoism or self-grasping may be one of the principal reifications that people make, but they are still only species while reification is the genus.

In *The Debate*, the one with reifying habits takes nine turns at talking. Each time, Lobsang Chögyi Gyalsten commences the passage with a reference like "The reifying habit replies...." On three such occasions—the first three instances in the text—Lobsang Chögyi Gyalsten uses the term "*bdag 'dzin*," perhaps to remain in conformity with the title of the text. On the six occasions that follow, which cover 90% of the text's volume, the text's antagonist is referred to by the name "*bden 'dzin*," which more specifically refers to apprehending entities to have inherent existence and bears no direct reference to a "self" or an "ego." Since there is only one antagonist for wisdom throughout the text, it is necessary that only one name be used for it; unlike most of the other options, "the reifying habit" is able to cover both of the Tibetan terms.

Another problem for the translation was that the dramaturgical formatting of the philosophical topics frequently has the reifying habit using the term "I" (*nga*) or "I myself" (*nga nyid*). Because reification has been anthropomorphized this way, giving the text its dramatic quality, it becomes necessary for the translator to select among three possible references for the "*nga*" – it is a triple entendre, as it were: (1) the habit of reifying the identifications one has made (2) the character who is functioning in the debate, and (3) an 'I' generally speaking. In English this polysemy cannot be rendered easily, making it necessary each time to select one among the three. Depending upon the context and the sense that is mostly implicated, all three of these ways to render "I" were used in a serial fashion; however, the thickness of the trope never really gets carried over into the English version.

Similar problems occurred with other key terms of the text, such as "truly existing," or "conventional existence."[16] "Truly existing" always references the presumption that an entity has an inherent essence, and initially it is necessary to qualify the term when it appears; but as the reader becomes more familiar with the meaning and usages of the term, one does not every time need to use so many words and it can be abbreviated without losing its intended function. "Conventional existence" is rarely referred to just that way. As provided in the previous footnote, more than a dozen words is needed to capture the full sense and reference of *tha snyad*. Fortunately, one needs to do that only once, and then one can select components of the lengthier definition, reducing the length and varying the lexical selection as the context requires, so that in the end the reader has received a full philosophical orientation to the notion. Naturally, every gain that a translation acquires has some associated cost. The least that one owes his readers is to avoid mindlessly repeating a phrase that is likely to remain unintelligible to most readers of English, an avoidance to which I gave high priority.

The chapter divisions, and sometimes the chapter titles, largely follow the divisions found in the Lobsang Jinpa commentary, which provides a classical section outline (see Appendix One). Section outlines for texts is one of the signal contributions to Buddhist hermeneutics developed by Tibetan scholarship. The Tibetans' section outlines afford readers a means to grasp the structure of the work as a whole, and also helps facilitate the relating of each component of the text to the other components.

Outline of the Book

The first chapter sets the tone of *The Debate*, while establishing the key issue that divides the two of them: the existence or non-existence of inherent essences and the way that such notions get objectified in everyday thinking. Many of the finest metaphors of Buddhist epistemology are introduced, in the course of which wisdom establishes his bona fides by citing Dharmakīrti, Śāntideva, and Aryadeva. Both wisdom and the reifying habit invite each other to depart the vicinity of the ordinary person's mind.

The one with reifying habits spends Chapters 2 through 4 satirizing a litany of the meditative practices of yogis and the philosophical tenets of some scholars (especially regarding the existence of an 'I') as limited, ineffective, and self-absorbed. Especially targeted are meditations that cultivate an inactive mind that attempts to stop engaging in thinking about anything at all. Making fun of some meditators, he announces, "I welcome all sky-like visions and all sky-like equipoises!" The reifying habit describes these meditations:

> Such meditation involves not losing oneself by chasing after what arises in the mind and instead remaining in a stable meditative equipoise. How is my way of obsessing about phenomena going to be harmed by a mind that never does anything! Incredibly, they label it "profound," but since no specific attention is being paid to the ego's lack of true existence, no damage will be done to me.

Wisdom replies by arguing for using analysis within a Mahayana meditative practice in which the philosophical themes and tantric themes are joined, whereupon the reifying habit criticizes such practices as being an addiction to overly analyzing matters, and the reifying habit characterizes these "wisdom" meditations as "a joke."

In a long soliloquy (Chapter 5), wisdom defends itself using some classical arguments from Tibetan dialectics, including an analysis of permanence and impermanence, the nature of everyday phenomena, and a description of interconnectedly dependent being. He poses to the one with reifying habits several classical dilemmas, including atomism. He asks how it can be possible for an 'I' to have a permanent essence and still take rebirth, and how "mineness" could have an independent existence apart from an 'I.' After exposing many contradictions in the reifying habit's position, wisdom wonders why the one with reifying habits is incapable of surrendering his belief in the true existence of his fabricated identities, and he asks him, "How is it that you are so very confident that this faulty notion of inherent being has absolute qualities that you will hold onto it no matter what?"

In Chapter 6, the reifying habit offers a highly comical inventory of many of the ways that persons become distracted from following wisdom's advice, a list that includes some preoccupations that may be familiar to readers. Wisdom responds in Chapter 7, and explains how appearance and emptiness, rather than being contradictory, are mutually dependent. A case is made for learning how to destroy the reifications that we construct out of what appears to us, and wisdom concludes the chapter with an elegant paean that consists of making offerings of six different philosophical realizations to the Buddhas, lamas, meditative guardians, et cetera.

In Chapter 8, the reifying habit cleverly rebuts wisdom's arguments by arguing that since wisdom would not have any object of meditation, or anything upon which emptiness can operate, unless some reification operates at the center of it, it is illogical to claim that reification has no existence. The reifying habit offers several more arguments in Chapter 9, which seem to prove that he must exist. His arguments appear to be perfectly logical, but each one is slightly off the mark, producing a very nice satire of logical argumentation. He also cleverly ridicules academic study in several pages that no scholar reading this book should overlook.

Those whose inclination is bent more towards meditative practice than to scholarly 'pursuits will not want to miss the reifying habit's ironic portraits of some of the more complicated meditative practices in Chapter 10 and at the beginning of Chapter 11. Anyone who has ever meditated will appreciate the accounts included in these pages. The latter part of Chapter 10 introduces a detailed analysis of some of the subtler aspects of higher tantric meditation, aspects that wisdom also elucidates, and remarkably so, in Chapter 11. In the final chapter (Chapter 12), the reifying habit argues that there is a gap between wisdom's words and the actual practices of cultivating wisdom, and then wisdom effectively explains the situation by offering a concise metaphor about the fire of wisdom requiring the fuel of reification, an illustration which has its origin in Nāgārjuna's *Fundamental Stanzas on the Middle Way*. Wisdom concludes by scolding the one with reifying habits, imploring him to seek the truth.

Not for a moment do the insights or wit slacken, making this text, which is more than three centuries old, something very contemporary.

---

[1] This title is descriptive of the text's content. Its full Tibetan title is *The Blazing Wheel of Thunderbolts That Split Asunder the Rocky Mountain of Egoistic Habits* (*bdag 'dzin gshags 'debs dgra dpung brag ri 'joms pa'i gnam lcags 'khor lo 'bar ba*). To reify a mental construction is to make it into a concrete thing.

[2] See Liberman 2013: 179-85, Chapter 6: "'There is a Gap' in the Tibetological Literature."

[3] The mandala with the celestial mansion is absorbed into the meditative deities who are joined in union; the consort is dissolved into the principal meditative deity, who is further absorbed into the seed syllable that sits on a sun-seat at his heart; finally, one element at a time each supporting component of the seed syllable dissolves into the graphic element that it supports until all that remains is the vertical "squiggle" of the NĀDA, which sits above the seed syllable. The NĀDA itself then dissolves into emptiness.

[4] The Tibetan here is *skhor gsum*, which literally means "three circles" and is a reference to having failed the three tests of a logically valid argument; however, its performative value is that one has defeated one's opponent in the debate. In a monograph on Tibetan philosophical debate, the translator translated this term as "Confounded by all three!" The "three" refers to (1) the opponent is unable to challenge the validity of the debater's reason; (2) the debater's reason applies in a pertinent way to the thesis (i.e., it has pervasion); and (3) the opponent cannot accept one's logical formulation without publicly demonstrating that he is being inconsistent with his earlier formal commitments. See Liberman 2004: 76, 161-62, 169-70, 238-43, and 277-78.

[5] See Peter Berger 1963: 41.

[6] The term "Absolute" is derived from Hegel; although it is inaccurate in the context of describing Tibetan epistemology, for Hegel it emerges only following a rigorous application of negative dialectics, so it is not as remote from the Mahayana "emptiness" as it may seem.

[7] For an introduction to the problem see Roger R. Jackson, "Deconstruction and Foundationalist Tendencies in Indian and Tibetan Buddhism," 2006.

[8] Literally, "thrusts and parries" is the nickname of the text, i.e. *gshags 'debs*.

[9] For a detailed analysis of an actual, extended Tibetan debate that examines this contradiction of having to formulate what is but cannot be formulated, consult a debate that was recorded from the Sera Je debating courtyard and transcribed verbatim, in Liberman 2004: 256-262.

[10] For an account of why the full particulars of thinking cannot be imagined and for some examples of what such *in vivo* descriptions look like, see Harold Garfinkel, 2002.

[11] These passages from *The Heart* Sutra and the *gsang ba 'dus pa* sadhana are my translations.

[12] *dmigs gtad mtshan 'dzin*, see text (p. 105).

[13] See Liberman 2013.

[14] *De dzhin du.*

[15] For a complete account of the considerations that went into the decision, please see Appendix Two.

[16] *Tha snyad du yod pa*, existing by virtue of a situationally contingent consensus regarding terminological conventions for understanding the local efficacy of a phenomenon.

Preamble to the Debate Between Wisdom and the Reifying Habit[1]

I offer my heart and my mind to my spiritual guides

The essence of the Great Mudra—including the profound *basis*, the spiritual *path* and its *result*—can be identified this way: throughout time all beings have been bogged down in an ignorance that has arisen naturally, without any solid basis, yet all the while the actual way of the mind's being has persisted along with it. This actual nature of the mind is the Great Mudra's profound *basis*, understood in the context of *sutra*.[2] Those who do not understand this will persist with their customary habits of fixating upon hypostatized "truths," which have to now led them to wander aimlessly in a repetitively superficial existence. The antidote to this ignorance is wisdom, which witnesses directly that every entity lacks independent, self-sufficient being. There is not a single other antidote to ignorance besides wisdom.

At the moment of their deaths, all beings from ants to the highest level of bodhisattvas experience the mother clear light. This also is the Great Mudra's profound *basis*, understood in the context of *tantra*. When the practice of stabilizing one's cultivation of this clear light intensifies and is sustained within a practice of meditative equipoise, it is the Great Mudra's spiritual *path.* Further, when the practice of wisdom is free from the proliferation of concepts and abides exclusively within its placement in equipoise, it is called "the view" of the path of the Great Mudra. When this manifests directly and unmistakably, even if temporarily, it is an aspect of the Great Mudra's result, and from the perspective of sutra it is called "the path of seeing" portion of the result.[3] Stabilizing and enhancing this cultivation of suchness is "the path of meditation," which is also considered "the path of training." After the subtlest of the obstructions to wisdom are purified, "the path of no further training" is reached and the *result* itself is actualized.

The Buddha has completely perfected the beneficial qualities, demonstrated abundant virtuous deeds, and recognized phenomena directly as if they were all simply an apple that rested in the palm of his hand. He abides unwaveringly in a body that has conjoined bliss with emptiness and never stirs from his recognition of suchness. To this state of being, the term "truth body" is applied. The truth body has its origin in the aspiration for a compassionate disposition, which is the basic resolve of every trainee. The truth body, the enjoyment body and the emanation body,[4] along with the paths, stages, and virtues (such as selfless service, etc.) are known to be nothing more than mere appearances, and nothing that exists inherently is ever evident.

---

[1] This title is descriptive of the text's content. Its full Tibetan title is *The Blazing Wheel of Thunderbolts That Split Asunder the Rocky Mountain of Egoistic Habits* (*bdag 'dzin gshags 'debs dgra dpung brag ri 'joms pa'i gnam lcags 'khor lo 'bar ba*). The author Lobsang Chökyi Gyaltsen (*blo zang chos kyi rgyal mtsan*) was the first person to become the Panchen Lama, although his lineage was retrospectively extended, making him the "Fourth" Panchen Lama.

[2] "Sutra" is a reference to the written records of the spoken teachings of the Buddha regarding morality, epistemology, and soteriology; it is here contrasted with "tantra," which are the subtle meditative practices that address transforming the underlying psychological, nervous, emotional, and sexual patterns that have taken root in one's mental continuum (the term "tantra" itself is a reference to that continuum), the habits of behavior that work beneath the level of discursive reflection. Knowledge regarding the practices of tantra is available only to initiates.

[3] The commentator Lobsang Jinpa explains, "Although in general the path of seeing is not the result, here the Great Mudra's result is taken to include everything from the path of seeing through the path of no further training." That is, the result referred to here includes the path of seeing, the path of meditation, and the path of no further training, all of which drive toward the result.

[4] *Chos sku, longs sku*, and *sprul sku*

1 The Debate Commences

Wisdom's injunction:

Among all falsehoods, the objectification of entities to which self-existence is wrongly ascribed is the greatest. Therefore, henceforth and for all time I renounce you, the reifying habit that fabricates things, the erroneous but obsessive concretizing of each entity one considers, including the ego. While there is no need for you to become disconcerted, you must leave this place and go somewhere else!

The one with reifying habits replies:

I have *always* accompanied the mind, no matter where it has gone. I'm the one who has constantly given it advice or scolded it, as needed. I have cared for it lovingly, in the way that a parent dearly loves a child; and I have provided it with both food and clothing. If I am not here to sustain desire and encourage greed, hatred, and ignorance, overwhelming any virtues that might threaten them, just who do you think is going to be able to keep all of these benefits coming?

Wisdom argues that the objects that the reifying habit reifies do not exist:

If since primordial time the mind has not for even one instant had any inherent self-existence, just exactly who is it that you think you were accompanying? Moreover, you yourself do not exist with any inherent essence; you are entirely without an independent being. So I must ask you *by whom*, and *to whom*, could your kind care and counsel have been given? Yes, do go away wherever you like, just as long as you don't return.

The reifying habit replies:

I may have no inherent existence, but the same applies equally to you! So I must ask you whose side it is that *you* can possibly be serving? If existing phenomena do not have even a speck of inherent essence, how can you posit anything, animate or inanimate? On the other hand, I come along in accordance with the mundane routines of conventional sense-making, so like yourself I can accept that there is no absolute being; however, if you deny that we have some existence in accordance with conventional notions you would be succumbing to a kind of nihilism, would you not?

It so happens that I am omnipresent throughout a wide range of contingent causes and results that involve interconnected relations and the mutual dependency of actors and their actions, but most of this time *you* have been missing-in-action! The self and I function perfectly well together in accordance with everyday customs, so it makes little sense for you to remain here with your ultimate truth, so go away yourself, and please do not bother to come back!

Wisdom replies:

Oh, it's for sure that you don't have an ultimate essence, you're right about at least that much. But since you don't have any inherent customary existence either, you are even unable to have an enduring effective influence over the fate of interconnectedly dependent phenomena, any of the reciprocal relations of actions and actors, or upon results and the causes that get linked to them. And if you wonder what is the reason, according to the habits of your way of thinking, functional phenomena exist by virtue of some inherent identifying essence without depending upon anything else. Such a self-nature would never be able to undergo further transformation; accordingly, its existence would be absolute, established as perfect reality, ultimate, existing in-itself, permanent, stable and enduring, with an indestructible nature that abides without change. Amidst a plenum like that, which is already so fully complete, it would be absurd for you to posit any role for yourself.

There is no place among the interconnectedly dependent relations—which are the episodic precipitates of the reciprocal being of actions and actors that are continuously influenced by adventitious causes and conditions—for anything to exist as permanently as you purport to exist. The independence of entities is contradicted by the fact that entities are always mutually dependent. The customary ways that you and I apprehend phenomena are as incompatible as are hot and cold.

This is the thinking of Dharmakīrti, who asserted in his *Commentary on Dignāga's Compendium on Valid Cognition*,[1] "If one does not refute everything that is inconsistent with what one has recognized to lack self-existent being, one will be unable to overcome obsessive reifications." Further, in *Engaging in the Practices of a Bodhisattva*,[2] Śāntideva explains, "Without some immanent contact with the objects that one imputes, one will be unable to appreciate precisely how it is that they lack inherent existence." And finally, *The Commentary to Aryadeva's Four Hundred Stanzas*[3] declares, "Any entity that depends upon nothing other than itself can be considered to have an inherent essence. But since no such entity exists, there is no self-existence."

For these reasons you and I are unable to coexist, and we will never be capable of doing so. So now be off to some other place! (267)

The reifying habit debates the extent of its association with the mind:

I have been the mind's companion for such an incredibly long time that I could not bear to be separated from it. I don't even know another other place where I could go! My home has been the very center of the heart, where I receive much affection. If the mind did not have me with it, it would become unable to desire anything effectively, and it would be unable to find all of the food and clothing that I help to provide! Moreover, the mind lacks the courage necessary for casting me out. If it dared to reject me, it would be left without its oldest friend, and it would not be able to make new friends so easily. Besides, it would be a very shameless thing for the mind to do, and if it did, it would surely suffer some unpleasant karmic consequences by doing so.

It would be a huge mistake to reject me on account of some newly befriended wisdom. Though many people have foolishly wished me to leave and have shouted, "Go away! Go away!" none of them has had any success at casting me aside. Since I provide so many blessings, no one is willing to drive me away. And if you should doubt this, consider the fact that even accomplished spiritual practitioners with considerable courage come to depend upon my blessings, and so they keep me close company until at least through the seventh level of a bodhisattva's evolution.[4] Indeed, the taste of my influence persists among bodhisattvas until they become fully accustomed to the final tenth level, so why even bother to consider the possibility of diminishing my influence upon ordinary folk?

This so-called "wisdom" arises only sporadically, whereas my friendship is continuous; hence, wisdom is unable to match me. Always accompanying me is a vast entourage that principally includes greed, hatred and ignorance but also envy, miserliness, deceit, arrogance, and the sixty-two false orientations such as pride, indolence, a lack of being conscientious, etc., all of which keep supplying the mind with a continuous stream of intense desires. Reducing my influence is indeed difficult; but trying to cast me out will be altogether out of the question.

While I am the mind's constant intimate companion, you, wisdom, are merely incidental. So if someone must leave, it is much more sensible that you be the one who does the departing. Your debating is mostly a lot of hot air, as if you were trying to blow hard on some dried yak dung in a kitchen stove in order to get it to flame up. Moreover, your message bears the conceit of a pair of deer's horns that, believing they arrived before the deer's ears, issue to the ears an order of expulsion. Because the mind's karma has developed together with my own, we are linked solidly; so even the Buddhas of the past, present, and future with all of their abilities and magical powers are unable to cast me out. If *they* are unable to do so, nothing can come of your fond dreams.

Wisdom refutes the arguments of the reifying habit:

You are like someone who wanders about searching everywhere for the very donkey on which he is riding. You are so fixated upon your own concretized thoughts that you are unable to recognize the way that things really are! Along with each being's mind abides a primordially pure nature, which is the enduring nature of sentient being; however, temporary defilements come along inadvertently and despoil that pure nature, covering them over. So, using your own illustrations, you yourself are the one who is trying to blow on the embers of the kitchen fire or like those horns that imagine they grew before the ears. I very much belong here; but just where your proper place may be, or where you could go to plant yourself, is anyone's guess. Although you say that you really belong here, the more that one investigates the matter, the more your shortcomings become apparent.

From the crown of the head to the tip of the toes, there is no truly existing self. An inherent self is not to be found among the five physical, mental, and emotional components of self-identity[5]—not in their aggregate nor in any of the individual parts. Nowhere does anything like you imagine exist. A thoroughgoing logical examination will establish that only interconnectedly dependent being exists, but I will save my discussion of this for later.

Nowhere does anything like you imagine exist, including yourself!—not among any of the individual components nor among all of them collected together. If you propose that the mind is the abode of the absolute self, please tell me in which instant of the mind it is that it dwells: in the instant that has just preceded, in the instant that immediately follows, or in the present instant? It is not in *any* of them, nor does it transcend them somehow; nor it is in any of the instants that preceded or succeeded those instants, not even in the most infinitesimal moment at the end of time. Not in any of these moments is there is an enduring self anywhere—and you yourself do not abide in the positive manner that you imagine you do! Furthermore, even if one should inspect each and every moment as carefully as one would count a hundred thousand hair-tips, one would be unable to discover there any mind that exists by virtue of possessing its own inherent nature. Investigation like this reveals your sorry self for just what it is.

The illusion that the self exists independently is thus destroyed, severed at its very roots, just as one might fell a poisonous tree. In this way, the dark penetrating obscurity of one's own ignorance, which has long been the master of one's thoughts, can at last be placed in its grave. When one cuts off this obscuring ignorance at its roots, that ignorance and all of the deluded phenomena that accompany it will be unable to regenerate themselves any further, and the mind's actual nature can be witnessed directly.

Since their origin, our objectifications have never had any inherent existence, essence, or fixed nature of their own. The mind's actual nature can be fully appreciated: a great free being. It witnesses, but does not fasten to anything it sees; it gazes, without concretizing what it gazes at; it meditates, without doing "meditation." It exists, but it is indescribable and exceeds objective labels or conceptions. Although its nature is to know, its knowing exceeds any labels and concepts. By deconstructing the ignorant habits of reifying the objects that it conceives, the mind can be freed from its own prisons. It silences the fanciful reifications of its notions and the continuous enumeration of its labels, rendering all of these entanglements a level plain in which everything has the same flavor. The events that compose our repetitive superficial existence (*samsara*) and those that compose an enduring reconciliation (*nirvana*) are indistinguishable for the reason that they are the same, identical events.

These are the consequences of any settling equipoise. From the vantage of absorption in such equipoise, all truth habits like yours—including even the notion of a Buddha—lack absolute being, and so too do the dharma, paths and stages of virtuous practitioners! Any spiritual results that manifest also lack inherent essence. There are no inherently true essences, so there cannot be any inherently false ones either.[6] If not even a *chos sku*[7] exists inherently, how in the world could you, the habit of reifying essences, possibly have inherent existence?

Surely, it is even less likely that the obscurantist self-delusions of common sense have true existence!

Following the completion of some concentrative absorption like this, the mind, whose basic nature is to be as empty as a mirror, simply reflects, without engagement, each obscurantist form that appears. These mere appearances have no enduring nature whatsoever; and no object bears an absolute, self-abiding truth. The mind, whose nature is empty and mirror-like, recognizes that whatever arises from the interconnectedly dependent relations of causes and conditions and manifests as hardened common sense is nothing more than a façade. If one never analyzes them, they may seem to exist; but when one subjects them to close scrutiny, they possess no inherent essence. These appearances acquire labels serendipitously, and one may adopt such customary identifications so long as one does no careful investigating, formulating "causes" and "effects" as if these two existed entirely independently of each other!

When one is no longer satisfied with superficial common sense understanding like that and investigates matters thoroughly, one will stop fabricating tidy explanatory schemes. Actors cannot exist independently of actions, and everywhere that there is an action there must also be an actor, so they are *reciprocally* determinative and not self-sufficient entities in the way that reifying them would have it. They are contingent phenomena that rely upon each other for their status. That mutually dependent phenomena should be made into truths that exist independently of each other is bizarre. That these truths are then made into absolutes is more incredible still! Though they are phantasms, concretizations like these eventually wear us out.

If we examine the case of a small child who ages and becomes elderly, that elderly nature seems to possess an intrinsic essence of its own; and somehow the pair of them—"the child" and "the elder"—each appear to us to be established independently of each other. But if this were so, then some elderly aspect would have to be evident in the baby even at the moment of its birth.

The mind's nature is to be as empty as the sky, but it soon grows overcast with the gathering clouds of the numerous notions that well up in illusory forms, resulting in a storm of activities that seem to be independently real, and somehow these causes and conditions precipitate like rain as concrete entities. No one recognizes that these notions have arisen from the mind itself. However, when they are analyzed carefully, they are discovered to develop much in the circumstantial way that clouds develop in the sky; and when our notions subside they do so in the way that a cloud, which may have appeared like a solid object, dissolves as it stretches across a clear blue sky. An able mind, on the other hand, is able to shed such dream forms as easily as an empty mirror casts back every image it receives.

When one becomes adept at ascertaining the interconnectedly dependent play of signification whereby the notions of "causes" and "effects" stabilize each other, one recognizes also how one has been lulled into a complacent acceptance of the patterns of thinking about "causes" and "effects" to which one has been habituated over a very long time. Then everything will be understood to be nothing more than appearances: thorough inquiry will cause one to awaken from this stupor and to recognize that the things that seem to have positive, independent existence do not really exist in the way that they appear. Although things still arise, their arising is related to the mind. Although things still subside, their subsidence is related to the mind. All results, and the actions related to them, are constructions built on the basis of these appearances.

Wisdom shines in the mind's emptiness, just as an image of the moon is reflected on the surface of an empty river.[8] Once one dispels the fog of wrong perspectives, one recognizes that everything that one cognizes is empty and has its dependent being in the same way that the moon appears in a river utterly empty of a moon; in that way wisdom appears in an utterly empty mind. Despite the fact that there are only appearances, we project essences everywhere in accordance with our conventional thinking; however, when one analyzes what is actually there, one does not observe any of these substantive essences. Moreover, whatever arises is derived from the nature of the mind; and whatever subsides dissolves into the mind's emptiness.

The phenomena that clamor in the natural emptiness of the mind resemble the echoes that resound from the face of a cliff. That is, our conceptual projections are loud proclamations of empty words that reverberate impressively, like echoes that have become separated from their origin. "Causes" and "conditions" are simply collections of echoes that cognition stitches together and announces abroad. Fortunately, ignorance like this is eliminated as easily as a lamp illuminates darkness.

Listen and reflect upon this: *upon analyzing them, appearances will be revealed to lack any abiding nature of their own.* Though things still arise, they arise from, and as, the nature of one's mind; though things still subside, they dissolve into, and as, the empty nature of the mind itself.

Your mode of apprehending phenomena and mine are completely contradictory, so it is simply impossible for us to reside alongside each other that way. That is why you must now go off to some other place!

---

[1] *Tshad ma rnam 'grel gyi tshig le'ur pa.*

[2] *Byang chub sems dpa'i spyod pa la 'jug pa.*

[3] The commentary to this seminal Middle Way text is by Candrakīrti, *Byang chub sems dpa'i rnal 'byor pa gzhi brgya pa'i rgya cher 'grel pa.*

[4] Of the ten levels of the progressive evolution of the career of a bodhisattva, the transition from the seventh to the eighth level is the most critical.

[5] According to Buddhist ontology, five components together comprise the existence of a sentient being; one of them is material and four of them are mental and emotional.

[6] This passage carries the implication that there could be inherently false ones only when it is the case that inherently true ones exist.

[7] From here forward, I am leaving the term *chos sku* in the Tibetan for the reason that the notion is so unfamiliar to readers of English that it is valuable not to facilitate a premature taming of the sense of the term "truth body" of a Buddha by repeating it too frequently in a facile way. This notion is often poorly understood, even though it operates at the heart of Buddhism and involves the most ultimate kind of realization and self-mastery; preserving the term's unfamiliarity here can be a hermeneutic advantage. The longer that the sense of the term can be suspended, the more extended its interrogation can be, and the more that readers stand to learn. Some translators use the Sanskrit term for translating *chos sku* into English, i.e. *dharmakaya*. While it does avoid the reduction of meaning that might occur by using an English term (there are no real cognates), it does not provide the reader any more clarity than using the text's own Tibetan term. Since this text is not a translation from Sanskrit but is an original Tibetan composition, I retain the term as used by the author.

[8] This illustration is helpful for emphasizing the way that nothing positive supports wisdom. Wisdom bear many traces of great significance, but there is no substance to any of them.

2 The Reifying Habit Ridicules Meditative Practices

The reifying habit defends itself:

Despite all your talk, as soon as I begin to promote the eight worldly concerns,[1] it will become evident that I have more influence than you do. Though your mode of apprehending phenomena and mine are indeed contradictory, in the end I'm the one who will be left standing! If we cannot live together here as friends, it makes more sense for you to be the one who looks for a new home.

I reside deep inside the human heart, whereas you come by only for an occasional unexpected visit. The friendship between the mind and I wavers as little as does Mt. Meru, the king of mountains, whereas your acquaintance brings to mind a momentary flash of lightning. My presence endures like the presence of an ocean, and the friendliness that people have for me is equally stable, without expansion or contraction, while your presence is nothing but an episode in a dream. You're the passing glint in an eye during a smile, whereas I'm the love that a mother always offers her child. You're a short-term visitor who, despite arriving from far away, tries to issue orders to vacate the premises.

The great meditators are a pathetic lot. They are so preoccupied with their various systems for meditation, which they claim cultivate the mind's real nature, that they are unable to discover any new insight that can transform their afflicted minds. They are unable to cut off the continuity of their previous mind or welcome any fresh mind. So they end up cultivating the same old mental ruts, which they never get beyond. Moreover, since these meditations are forms of self-absorption they end up being mostly about me! As remedies, your sorts of meditations are ineffective for combatting my habits of reifying thoughts, so how can they inflict any damage upon me? You won't be able to lay a finger on me!

There are some meditations that involve cultivating an inactive mind that for a time ceases to engage in thinking of anything at all. These meditations are in no way incompatible with my habit of developing conceptual fixations, so they too are unable to inflict any harm upon me. How could such meditations amount to anything? They will be unable to touch me!

There are some meditations that make a thorough search for the mind's form and fail to locate a thing, but this problem has nothing to do with me. How is a failed search like that going to impede the successful way that I conceive of things? And since it accomplishes nothing for your side, you need to explain how it will be able to damage me.

There are some meditations that cultivate the immanent flow of the bare mind, but meditations like that become merely instances of the mind meditating on the mind itself, and they never get around to the business of confronting me directly. Besides, all meditations on the 'I' are basically friendly to me anyway, so how will your meditations be able to do me any harm? They will not lay a hand on me!

There are some meditations of "vast awareness,"[2] during which one cuts off each appearance the very moment that it arises, including specific meditative content of any kind that may develop. They too could not possibly do a whit of harm to me, since they offer no effective countermeasures for combating my habits of producing conceptual fixations. These meditations will come to nothing, and so they too will be unable to touch me. Meditating without considering any instruction about the nature of reality leads only to some facile identification of anything and everything as being perfectly wonderful, and to mouthing dry words like "Wow" or "This is really fine!" that are proudly imagined to bear great profundity. Most of those who practice equanimity this way are actually cultivating me inside of their meditations, so these practices have little consequence for my existence.

There are some meditations known as "Meditation-on-the-non-existence-of-an-'I'." The lack of inherent existence of an 'I' is not equivalent to utter non-existence, yet many practitioners have not learned to distinguish these two correctly and so end up cultivating the view of utter non-existence. When they meditate this way, it only furthers my purposes. They never reach the point of analyzing in the way that is required. Those kinds of effective analyses are missing; they do not make an appearance, even for an instant. The very idea that I should be the one to leave makes me laugh out loud.

The meditations that you yourself advocate, which do consider instructions about the nature of reality, are fully occupied with a vast plethora of proofs for the true existence, or the lack of true existence, of one extreme or another; these endless investigations foster a manic searching for analytic flaws, which eventually wears down any meditator. This searching for formal analytic faults will continue even during placement meditation! What kind of meditation can be accomplished so long as these endless examinations persist? Even the analyzer must be analyzed, as well as the analyzing that analyzes that! Since the "antidote" of analytic meditation is never able to complete its tasks, it analyzes endlessly, and the meditator becomes trapped within a massive net of concepts, which is greatly fatiguing and offers scarce opportunity for genuine meditation. While these analyses are under way, they seem to be very important, but when it becomes time for practicing a stabilizing meditation, the practitioner doesn't have a clue about what to do. That's when some practitioners end up meditating upon me! At other times they meditate on utter nothingness. Still other meditations involve indiscriminately cutting off every thought that may arise. Legitimate meditations that settle the mind upon a proper object,[3] and by doing so undermine my habit of reifying the 'I,' are extremely rare. With methodologies like these, practitioners will be unable to get past their own limitations, so please don't tell *me* to get out!

Wisdom, you are as rare as the Giant Lotus.[4] Perhaps once, for a brief time, your efforts may be efficacious, but that is only after one has devoted an endless eon to assembling great collections of profound wisdom and superior merit, thereby pleasing one's lama. I don't have to work nearly that hard, yet I am the master who continues to reign.

In order to remove me you must cultivate a flawless wisdom that is able to act as an antidote that undermines my habits of reifying the ego, which conceive the ego to exist with an inherent essence. Except for realizing this right sort of errorless wisdom, the other "antidotes" that get employed are incapable of producing any real conviction. Hence, they merely assist me and serve my interests, and are unable to free anyone. Meditations that keep trying to sort out precisely, "This one exists," "That one does not exist," and that sort of thing are unable to suppress me; likewise impotent are meditations that cultivate a consciousness that is free from conceptions, which they do while constantly aiming to focus upon the way that things really abide. Ho-ho! That one especially gives me a hearty laugh.

There are some meditations that involve concentrating upon cognizing the empty nature of whatever appears to the mind, appearances that are then abandoned. These empty appearances are taken to be illusions, and these practitioners cultivate an awareness of the lack of inherent existence in any of them. I'm willing to grant you that these are genuine meditations; however, their efficacy extends only to a handful of the shortcomings of conventional kinds of everyday thinking.

When performed well, they are able to address the nature of a few common illusions, but they never address the fundamental nature of reality. Only when one meditates on how the 'I' itself lacks any basis whatsoever can there be an opportunity to inflict real damage upon me. That is, as soon as one appreciates that the 'I' has no inherent being, it cannot continue to exist in the way that reification has concretized it. So long as one fails to cultivate a targeted examination of the lack of the inherent existence of the 'I,' the habit of reifying an inherently existing ego cannot be combated effectively. So how can harm come to me by employing such a general practice of meditative cultivation?

There are some meditations that consider the mind to have a sky-like emptiness with neither external limits nor a center. I heartily welcome all sky-like visions and all sky-like equipoises! It is ridiculous to think that a sky not having limits or a center can raise any doubts at all regarding my habit of concretizing an 'I.' Moreover, if a mind, being formless, has no boundaries, center, or ascertainable limits, then neither do I, since I assume my stature on the basis of the mind; hence, it follows that I am untouchable too! Accordingly, meditative antidotes like these are misguided.

There are some meditations that focus upon stray thoughts that slip in, to which one tries to apply a bit of mindfulness. The practitioner observes these like someone who is watching a spectacle: "Oh look at that one!" Though it is the nature of such thoughts to disappear on their own, when they do disappear, the situation is misidentified as the practitioner having just achieved the *chos sku*[5] itself, when in fact it is nothing more than a few random conceptualizations that have finally exhausted themselves on their own. If they are the *chos sku*, then *chos sku* would become plentiful; and without anyone having developed much capacity to control their thoughts, one could claim to have achieved the rarely obtained *chos sku* that realizes suchness! Such practitioners mistake their meditations for meditations upon the mode of being of reality itself. Thoughts may have no identifiable form, and neither may the mind, but notions such as these do not effectively combat my customary way of identifying the 'I'. Since those methods are incapable of cultivating a view of the actual way of reality, it is ludicrous to speak about their witnessing the *chos sku*. Your notion of me being the one to depart is equally laughable.

There are some meditations that undertake comprehensive investigations into whether any phenomenon that exists does so as an individual or as a plurality.[6] Anything that exists inherently must exist in one of those two possible ways. After much thorough study, this method of meditation fails to locate anything that exists in either manner. Unfortunately, here one is meditating only upon the presence of the reason [i.e., not existing inherently as an individual or as a plurality] in the subject [a phenomenon], so it does not address my own lack of inherent existence nor does it cultivate any non-existence of the 'I,' which is the specific matter that is under discussion here.[7] Since it does not directly confront the habit of reifying the 'I,' it is not a meditation upon my lack of true existence.

There are some meditators who, when analyzing whether a phenomenon exists as an individual or as a plurality and not finding either mode of existence, think the 'I' exists as nothing more than a projected notion; however, this analytic meditation is simply an affirming negation,[8] so it still leaves some scope for inherent existence. Since it is not a non-affirming negation, which would afford no place at all for me to dwell, it does not entirely undermine my habit of reifying the 'I.' If it is unable to contradict the habit of reification, then what is going to compel me to depart? Since it cannot damage the ego, how does wisdom think it is going to be able to prevail?

These meditators who undertake a thorough analysis of a phenomenon's non-existence as an individual or as a plurality and discover no such entity come to convince themselves, "Now I am meditating on emptiness," and they settle into some contemplation, but a superficial exercise like that is a far cry from being an effective cultivation of emptiness. The sort of emptiness that these practitioners focus upon has little chance of leading them to cultivate the emptiness of inherent essences. Though such persons may be contemplating some kind of emptiness before them, they fail to employ the correct methodology for realizing the profound emptiness.[9] Wisdom, which is the only effective antidote against me, quickly eludes these practitioners who have no precise realization. Since they lack the proper antidote, how can they accomplish anything? Consequently, it remains suitable for me to keep residing here.

There are some meditators who, when investigating whether a phenomenon exists as an individual or as a plurality, undertake their analyses with meticulous detail. They consider it "investigating whatever passes before one" or "deconstructing the objectivated idea that is the focal point for reflection." Such meditation involves not losing oneself by chasing after what arises in the mind and instead remaining in a stable meditative equipoise. How is my way of obsessing about phenomena going to be harmed by a mind that never does anything? Incredibly, they label it "profound," but since no specific attention is being paid to the ego's lack of true existence, no damage will be done to me. "Wisdom" meditation like that is a joke!

When some meditators who analyze whether a phenomenon exists either as an individual or as a plurality fail to locate anything of the sort, they try as much as they can to convert the mental state that results from their logical inferences about the lack of inherent existence into a placement in enduring equipoise. This is somehow construed to be "profound meditation on things' actual mode of being," when it is really only a species of conventional understanding. They mistake their own cultivation of some mundane conceptualizations for a grasp of the actual mode of being of phenomena. Ho-ho! What an idiosyncratic "wisdom" that is! Anyone who meditates this way is my very good friend. These meditations, which investigate carefully whether the 'I' has any truly existing essence in the form of an individual or a plurality and ascertain that it does not, simply mistake the mental continuum that emerges from this kind of ascertainment for a profound equipoise on the way that things are ultimately. As a matter of fact, obsessing about a conceptual ascertainment that way is not all that different in its structure from the habits that I myself regularly practice, so how in the world will such a method be capable of reducing these conceptual fixations? Since it is just another way to cultivate me, how will it be able to cultivate wisdom?

There are some meditators who, after analyzing carefully, conclude that the 'I' does not have any truly existing inherent essence as an individual or as a plurality, but they fail to cultivate a correct understanding of non-existence; instead, they search in places that are remote from actual emptiness and devise a notion that is something different from what emptiness really is, one that comes perilously close to nihilism. Further, they turn their notion of emptiness into one more truth habit, which their mind then fixates upon, so it becomes merely another way to cultivate what is consistent with my standard operating procedure. Consider carefully whether that could ever come to serve as a proper antidote for the obsessive reifying that I regularly practice. Because you never have a decent hold of what the non-existence of inherent essence really is, the emptiness that you come upon is remote from the profound emptiness. No matter how many may mouth the words, very few really cultivate the non-inherent existence of the 'I.'

Some of those meditative practitioners who investigate carefully whether the 'I' has any truly existing inherent essence in the form of an individual or a plurality ascertain that it does not, but they then fixate obsessively on that ascertainment itself. So far as possible, they abide there in a placement meditation, and they may even mistake their infatuation with their own concepts for being a meditation on ultimate being. A few of them may actually cultivate a bit of emptiness and cause me some harm; however, there is no way they will be able to inflict any terminal damage.

The reason for this is as follows. The very notion of 'I,' which is merely an idea that is projected upon a collection of mental, emotional, and physical components, generates egoistic thinking. The stronger that an 'I' gets conceived, the more concrete it becomes, until it seems to exist in truth. Such egoistic reflections lead to objectifications that become truth habits, and what acquires an appearance of truth that way is then further reified as a truth-in-itself. In this manner whatever appears to the mind is accepted to be true, existing independently in just the way it has been concretized; and this habit persists as a subtle defect even for those bodhisattvas who have evolved to the final tenth level, a defect that is well known by the label, "subtle obscurations." Because of this, in the period following a master's meditative absorption on emptiness, what merely appears to be real is still taken for real, although it no longer becomes an obsessive fixation. Of course, during the absorption of an active meditative equipoise, neither subtle nor obsessive ways of reifying existence occur; moreover, a Buddha never alternates between equipoise and post-equipoise mental states, and neither the subtler nor the grosser obscurations are ever manifest. For ordinary people, however, both types of obscuring reifications are fully operative. The thought of the 'I' arises on the basis of the aggregated total of one's mental and physical components, and this 'I' appears to truly exist.

When, on the basis of analysis one ascertains that it does not exist as an individual nor does it exist as a plurality of these components and that there is no truly existing 'I' at all, for a time one may be able to sustain the mental continuum that follows from this way of apprehending, but this sort of ascertainment can harm me only a little. Why is that? For the reason that during the process of refuting the true existence of the notion of 'I' that is supported by the aggregated mental, emotional, and physical aspects of a human being, each of these individual aspects themselves still get reified. Accordingly, the appearance of the true existence of an 'I' based upon them will retain an opportunity to reappear, and there will always be the potential for egoism to rise anew. No matter how much one may meditate on the lack of true existence of each one of the five principal mental, emotional, and physical components, or on the 'I,' the habitual mode of fixating upon "reality" will never be contested directly in an immanent or effective way, and so the 'I' that was objectivated on the basis of the components will still appear to exist truly. While any formal analysis that deconstructs what appears to be true that way may find such an ascertainment convincing for a while, it will not have very enduring effects. Even after one has employed a non-affirming negation, i.e., one that refutes only the inherent existence of such an objectivated 'I' on the basis of the aggregated components without suggesting the true existence of anything else, various objects that were reified will retain their capacity to exercise effective action.

Both lethargy and mental excitement may be avoided, conceptual reifications may be destroyed, some skill achieved in sustaining a mode of perceiving phenomena without reifying an 'I' on the basis of the aggregated components, and some ability to keep me at bay can come about; however, this happens very infrequently, and in most circumstances some form of a fixed 'I' will persist. Some practitioners keep striving to expel me even though no one has ever been able to set eyes on me, and this presents them with an impossible task. Their strategies are very much like those who carry their protection money to the western door for the purpose of placating a demon who sits at the eastern door. They are trying to identify a thief they have never seen, trying to hit a target with an arrow without bothering to look at where they are aiming; they are fools who believe they have finally fulfilled their dream of discovering precious jewels, even though they are unable to distinguish a jewel from an ordinary stone. Wisdom, I'm sorry to inform you that what you think you are inspecting during your meditations is not really the profound thing that you think it is! All this while I remain in charge, the sole means by which the mind is able to achieve its happiness.

Some who keep telling me to go away employ the formal analytic strategies that make up the Seven-Fold Reasoning, which seeks to sustain a mode of discerning that ascertains that an 'I' that arises on the basis of the physical, emotional, and mental components and seems to be an object in-itself has no true existence in reality.

When consciousness apprehends the world that way, in what is called "sustaining the discernment," it is still cultivating my kind of truth habits, only on a more subtle level. The practice will not become effective at undermining the ego since the techniques it employs constitute only another variety of mental constructions that obscure reality. Simply announcing, "There is no inherent essence!" by itself can never inflict serious injury, though from time to time it might cause me some small difficulty.

There are several varieties of what is called a non-affirming negation. For instance, there is an empty sky that has no center or borders. But how is it that contemplating something that has no limits or center, being formless, and never directing one's attention to me directly, will become a practice that perceives things in ways that can undermine me? It does not come close to damaging me. Similarly, you often criticize the way people look up at a great snow mountain and think that it is blue[10] or how they see the sky and say, "It is blue," but you never address directly any actual existence of the sky or the mountain. How can such a generalist perspective undermine the specific ways that people habitually apprehend things? The idea that your discernment will cause me any harm makes me laugh.

It is for sure that you have refuted that the sky has any substantial dimension that one can make contact with, but that is the only thing you have done. Which mental continuum is that able to affect? It may be a discernment, but even when you sustain that discernment it will leave the cultivation of my essence in tact. Consequently, obsessive reification will not be undermined in the slightest way. When you keep crying, "It lacks inherent essence," even there a notion is still being employed. Is the mental continuum that sustains that notion the same one as the mental continuum that ensues from a non-affirming negation itself, or is it different from it? If it is not the same, then we need to examine the situation more carefully.

What we have been speaking of as the non-affirming negation that is the sky, which lacks any substantial dimension with which one can make any actual contact, involves a label that is imputed. Similarly, the higher ascertainment that is associated with the mental continuum of a non-affirming negation that deconstructs the notion of truly existing essences can itself become objectified and entail a praxis of reification! Oh sure, it has a robust life, but only as another named and imputed notion, i.e. "non-affirming negation," which gets thought while one is analyzing suchness. And with a vague label like this in hand, one then attempts to place oneself into equipoise. Beyond its name, such a notion is obscure, ambiguous, lacking in clarity, and without any sharp focus or potency; it is muddled, continually vacillating, weak, diffused, and at some times even spaced-out. As a matter of fact, I myself provide you some of these notions that leave you wondering what they could have been about. You sit mostly in dumb surprise, unable to put together a decent understanding that can give you any certainty about just what they might be. This way I'm able to completely exhaust you. While you go on adhering to these misguided notions, I keep sending you more of these same blessings; meanwhile, beneath your cerebrations I nap peacefully, and no harm comes to me while I do.

Not only is the 'I,' which is objectified on the basis of the aggregated mental and physical aspects, not abandoned when you undertake your analyses that refute true existence, the 'I' is also fully operative while you are stabilized in equipoise. You constantly conceive more of these concretizations and seem to be unable to let go of them! The mental continuum of a non-affirming negation is supposed to be capable of undermining the exercise of such truth habits and establish a seat of undistracted equipoise that, when cultivated to a point of great familiarity, is the accomplishment of wise ones; however, obtaining that sort of force and clarity is exceedingly rare. In the meantime I'm able to relax here quite comfortably, and for a very long spell.

Wisdom, you seem very exercised about all of this, but you shouldn't wear yourself out about it since all of these great meditations will in the end conform to my way of thinking anyway. It would be better for you just to relax peacefully without being troubled, in a way that more befits your nature.

Although you keep telling me to get out, you remain incapable of inflicting any damage upon me. If you want to know the reason, then listen to me carefully. Generally speaking, all sentient beings obey me faithfully like they were devoted subjects. There may be a few who yearn for liberation, but after I have finished hurling my five arrows of afflicted minds at them,[11] there is nothing that even master practitioners can do to salvage their liberation. Some practitioners of meditation are guided by philosophical tenets and others are not. Those with philosophical training are exceedingly rare, and even they may be divided into two camps—the ones who follow Buddhist tenets and others who follow outsiders' tenets. Moreover, the latter greatly outnumber the former, and they have countless tenets, which are either naively positivist or nihilist, and neither perspective is able to offer any assistance.

There are nihilists such as the worldly materialists[12] who think this is their only life and accept no earlier or subsequent births. They even deny the possibility of liberation and the efficacy of the three jewels,[13] etc. These practitioners accept that the present self simply exists and perishes, and they reject every possibility of liberation or omniscience. On the other hand, there are other, positivist practitioners, such as the Enumerators[14] who classify all phenomena into twenty-five ontological categories. They accept the possibility of liberation but reject omniscience, and they even hold that it is possible for some created things to be permanent! [15]

There are other non-Buddhist sects who have perfected the four practices of concentration[16] and even acquired a capacity for extra-sensory perception, magical powers, etc. But their assiduous cultivation of such outlooks does not enable them to acquire the capacity to endure the fear of experiencing emptiness, nor are they able to make progress toward attaining even the psychic heat or peak of fortitude levels.[17] Since none of these practitioners manage to cultivate any wisdom, how will I suffer any difficulties? Feelings, discriminative identifications, and ideation may be rendered inactive, and one can cut also off anything that appears to the mind, spend eons meditating in an apathetic stabilized equipoise, and still not be effective at inflicting any harm upon me. It is a view of utter nothingness. Such yogis eliminate whatever discriminative identifications pop into their heads. But since no wisdom can be cultivated this way, even if they meditate for an eon like that I will escape any harm.

There is a view that makes no discriminations at all. According to how they cultivate it, they hold that discriminations neither exist nor do they have non-existence. They meditate mindlessly this way without any thoughts of existence or non-existence: even if they were to meditate like this for an eon, they would not affect me in the slightest, since they are incapable of cultivating any antidotes that are effective. Oh sure, this is the great view that is well known as neither-existence-nor-non-existence![18] Meditators like that do not rely upon the slightest signifying form and eliminate anything that comes to mind; they exclusively entertain "clear and knowing"[19] reflections. In that way they cultivate a stabilized equipoise that endures for many eons. By eliminating the opportunity for any of the conditions that cause suffering to manifest, such a consciousness may eliminate the suffering of change and the suffering of suffering; nevertheless, it is incapable of eliminating the all-pervasive suffering. It abides in whatever formlessness happens to settle upon one, but that is not a corrective that can destroy me or my interests. Wisdom, it appears that no matter what sort of these meditations you attempt, you keep failing to get beyond these formless perceptions.

These days the vast majority of meditation is "meditation" in name only and consists of little more than some sweet composure with a bit of added pious chanting. They may try their best, and those who meditate this way may think there is no meditation better than what they practice; however, there is no way that it is going to lead them to realizations about my ultimate non-existence. The way that you and I—wisdom and reification—apprehend the world is utterly incompatible, and so any meditative practice that fails to take on explicitly the manner in which I conceive things will never be capable of cultivating a practice that can destroy me. Only a practice that confronts me directly, in the same way that light dispels darkness, will work; no other methodology can become an effective remedy. Only when one destroys the essentialism that transforms the aggregated physical, emotional, and mental aspects of being into a reified concept will the mind that fixates upon them be eradicated and the correct outlook upon reality be adopted.

---

[1] Seeking possessions, fearing any loss of possessions, desire for fame, the wish to avoid becoming unpopular, seeking praise, wanting to avoid criticism, savoring pleasure, and avoiding misery.

[2] *Rig pa zang thal.*

[3] The lack of inherent essences is an illustration of a proper object of meditation.

[4] *Ficus clomerata*, a rare lotus of immense size.

[5] See Chapter 1, footnote 7, p. 57.

[6] This is a well-known complex of logical analyses that proves the lack of inherent existence by establishing that there is no true essence that exists either as a singularity or in concert with other entities [*bden grub du gcig dang bden grub gi thun mong gang rung dang bral ba*].

[7] Here the argument of the reifying habit is that this is only a demonstration of the correctness of the reason, and not a logical pervasion or a proof. This is similar to the statement, "All horses [subject] are cows [thesis] because they have four legs [reason]," which includes a subject that possesses the reason without any proof that is applicable to the thesis. The argument may show that a certain phenomenon has no inherent existence, but it does not demonstrate that the habit of reifying the 'I' in particular is such a phenomenon. Accordingly, it does not supply a pertinent logical pervasion. Here Panchen Lobsang Chögyi Gyaltsen is reviewing the "Four Great Reasonings" of Middle Way analysis.

[8] That is, it bears the implication that there is something else that does exist. In negating one thesis an affirming negation implies the existence of another thesis that implicates that there is still some true existence; hence, reification can survive the analysis. On the other hand, if there were a total denial of an 'I,' it would become a form of nihilism. The argument that the one with reifying habits is making here is a simulation of common Tibetan debating strategies.

[9] There is some conflict over how to interpret this analysis of non-existence as an individual or as a plurality. The author of a major Sera Je college textbook, Jetsun Chögyi Gyaltsen (1469-1546), argues that it does constitute an effective proof of emptiness, whereas the author of an important textbook from Drepung Monastic University's Loseling College, Panchen Sonam Drakpa (1478-1554), argues that it is not an effective proof. In his Mahāmudrā text Lobsang Chögyi Gyaltsen seems to take the former position, whereas here he seems to be adopting the latter position.

[10] When one looks at the glaciers on a high mountain, they have a blue sheen, even though the ice of the glacier itself is not really blue.

[11] The five arrows are dull wittedness, cravings, complete obscuration, yearning, and mortality.

[12] The Cārvāka.

[13] The three jewels are the Buddha, the doctrine (Dharma), and the spiritual community (Saṃgha).

[14] The Sāmkhya.
[15] Shiva and Brahma are examples of permanent entities.
[16] Such as Jaiṇs.
[17] Psychic heat and the peak of fortitude (which entails the irreversibility of one's attainments) are the first and second levels of the Path of Preparation. The fear is experienced during the third of the four levels of the Path of Preparation.
[18] "*Yod min med min*," is a view associated with a number of non-Gelug adepts such as the Sakya master Gorampa Sonam Senge (*Go rams pa bsod nams sen ge*, 1429-1489; see, for instance, Gorampa nd: 50) and the Nyingma master Longchenpa (*kLong chen rab 'byams*, 1308-1364; see Longchenpa 2001: 18).
[19] "Clear and knowing" is the definition of the pure mind according to Mahāmudrā, Lobsang Chokyi Gyaltsen's own tradition of practice.

3 The Reifying Habit Criticizes the Lower Schools of Philosophical Tenets

The reifying habit continues:

Hinayana methods of meditation like those of the Vaibhāśika consider it sufficient to visualize consciousness pared down to its basic aspects of knowing and being unobstructed, but their meditations upon this luminous mind only reinforce their idea that a consciousness truly exists, so this practice is not much of a strategy for doing damage to me. Their powerfully stabilized equipoise is focused upon the tiniest pieces of atoms that exist without having even directional parts. These atoms touch nothing, nor is anything affixed to them, although they come extremely close to touching each other. All these inconsequential appearances that fill up the meditators' minds are meaningless, and they only leave the meditators exhausted. Without any visible substance these atoms somehow combine together to form mountain ranges, or walls and houses that consist mostly of space, so they would seem to be incapable of obstructing anything. If that were so, it should be an easy matter to leave one's footprints and handprints even on stones!

No doubt these contemplative practices possess immeasurable virtues; however, since none of them involve directly contradicting my way of conceiving things, they remain ineffective efforts. When the majority of these great contemporary meditators attempt to cultivate all of these details, they delude themselves into thinking that they are fabulous practitioners. Just how is one going to gain wisdom with this kind of conceit? Quite the contrary, it is only further perpetuation of my egoistic method of conceiving things, and so they offer not the slightest opposition to my ways. When they practice like that they may be able to generate a foundation for developing a sincere admiration for emptiness; nevertheless, they are unable to set aside the many truth habits that go about reifying everything in just the manner that I am used to conceiving them. Moreover, they fear that if one should repudiate these truth habits, it would become impossible for them to correctly formulate the phenomenal relations of cause and effect, or the relations between actors and actions. Once they accept this fear, which is consonant with my own thinking, any hope of harming me will be lost.

There are also the Hearer Vehicle practitioners known as the Followers of Sutra.[1] No matter how much they cultivate a stabilized equipoise that focuses on their topics, they will be unable to reach the first two stages of the path of preparation, i.e. psychic heat and the peak of fortitude. Accordingly, attaining the final stage of only the path of preparation—the capacity to endure the fears that accompany the direct experience of emptiness—is out of reach for them altogether.

Among the Mahayanists, the Mind-Only[2] and Formal Analytic Reasoning-based Middle Way practitioners[3] contend that phenomena exist through the force of some essence that abides within phenomena,[4] by means of characteristics that generate themselves,[5] by virtue of an inherent nature they bear; they further accept that their existence is substantive. And they even imagine that they prove all of this through formal analysis!

Mind-Only practitioners in particular subscribe to a form of positivism, according to which they accept that some entities[6] have an existence that is truly real, and so they cultivate a view that incorporates this positivism. By doing so, not only do they fail to harm me, they end up making me the centerpiece of their meditation! Therefore, their meditations are quite friendly to me. They fear that one who denies that there are any inherent essences will be unable to account properly for cause and effect, a situation that they think would make it extremely difficult to secure liberation and offers no scope at all for gaining omniscience; further, they think such denial would undermine the authority of conventional and ultimate truths, which serve as the bases for liberation. Nāgārjuna himself speaks about this, and I will even cite the passage for you: "Non-Dialectical School practitioners have no proper method for accomplishing complete pacification. The actuality of customary truths is undervalued, thereby undermining the two truths and making liberation impossible."[7]

In a similar case, the Formal Analytic Reasoning-based Middle Way School practitioners,[8] who reject the view that any entities have real existence, nevertheless contend that entities do exist by means of characteristics that generate themselves. But if standard conventions were not at all real, one would not know how to formulate any of the reciprocal relations between actors and actions or between causes and effects. They have not discarded such perspectives, and it is unlikely that they will generate a mental continuum suitable for the path of the master sages who practice the most difficult of all the paths of the three vehicles.[9] Even the most refined of the practitioners run aground at this point, unable to progress beyond elementary realizations.

Most accomplished meditative practitioners have not studied or understood anything efficacious, and instead develop minds that inhabit an ignorant darkness. In such pitch darkness they are capable of walking straight into a wall. When the mind engages nothing whatsoever, there can be no mindfulness, nor can there even be anything that can rightly be called a "view" or "meditation," so there will be no way for such practices to undermine my way of conceiving things. If they have not retained a close familiarity with the *actual* bare primordial characteristics of the mind—its clarity and its having the capacity to know—they will mistake the blankness of their undistracted stabilized equipoise, which cuts off anything that comes to mind, for the utmost realization of the mind's primordial characteristics. When they meditate this way there can be no obtaining liberation. The idea that such practitioners could attain omniscience is a matter worthy of ridicule. Believing that the practice of cutting off anything that arises in the mind is equivalent to the meditation that realizes the bare clarity and knowing nature of the mind is a prescription for becoming self-obsessed with the conventional existence of one's own mind. Since this conventional mind shares its identity with the 'I,' one will be unable to leave egoism behind. The result of cultivating me in this way is that liberation will never be obtained, and I will grow more fulsome. For me it does not get any better than this!

The most esteemed among those known as Middle Way practitioners—those who follow the Negative Dialectics School—contend that the only view that bodhisattvas reliably witness is that of some post-meditative attainments.[10] For the Buddha on the other hand, there is no difference between meditative absorption and post-meditative activity. Dialecticist practitioners believe that everything that exists does so only as the outcome of the names and situational conventions that are projected, whereas none of these nominal objectifications are operative at the level of the Buddhas; nor is there any reality to the dualism of meditative absorption and post-meditative attainments, as is explained in Maitreya's *Uttaratantra* and similar texts.

Wisdom briefly dismisses the reifying habit:

Mere faith in my viewpoint pacifies all of a person's emotional afflictions; on the other hand, anyone who sustains gnawing doubts about me will soon find their life in tatters. The briefest reflection will leave no doubts about the need for you to exit the scene. Cultivating and reflecting upon my nature naturally leads to obtaining liberation, whereas you offer up nothing more than endless cycles of disastrous behavior, which is the real enemy. Anyone who fails to drive you out completely will face a repetition of destructive cycles of behavior that never seems to end.[11]

---

[1] Sautrāntika.

[2] Cittamātrā.

[3] Svātantrika Madhyamaka.

[4] *Ngo bo nyid gyis grub.*

[5] *Rang gi mtsan nyid gyis grub.*

[6] This is a reference to thoroughly-established phenomena (*yong grub*), ideas that have overcome dualism, and to the Mind-Only School's notion that a fundamental all-pervading consciousness truly exists.

[7] The Negative Dialectics School is the Prāsangika (Skt.) or *Thal 'gyur pa.* The citation is actually from Candrakīrti, *Dbu ma la 'jug pa*, Chapter Six. Not only is the one with reifying habits misattributing the passage, he is misinterpreting it. The Panchen Lama's misattribution and misinterpretation here is possibly deliberate, a satirical form in which the critic in the drama (here the one with reifying habits) is being satirized.

[8] Svātantrika Madhyamaka. The Panchen Lama here characterizes this school as being composed of a mixture of nihilism and positivism.

[9] That is, the Mahayana; the three vehicles are the Hearers, Solitary Realizers and the Great Vehicle practitioners.

[10] If they did have a view during their actual ultimate realization, it would necessarily involve the imputation of names and meaning, which would disqualify it from being ultimate. This addresses a deep irony that necessarily operates at the heart of Middle Way philosophical and meditative practice.

11 The commentary by Lobsang Jinpa further elucidates these destructive cycles of behavior (Jinpa nd: 34-35):

> Although reifying egoistic habits may hold sway for a while, I will learn how to cast them aside. They bring about conflicts between people and fuels their debates and recriminations. They lead them to criticize each other, thus promoting divisiveness. I prefer to possess excellent qualities, pleasing speech, a good reputation, and the finest bliss and happiness, all of which are undermined by the habitual behaviors that are formed while one has contempt for others, pride, and the least bit of impatience or jealousy.
>
> If one cannot tolerate hearing even a hint of insult, one will become hostile. When one is overly concerned with how other people are looking at one, good or bad, other people will become one's enemy, and there will be no harmony in any of one's relations. If that happens, there can be no harmony between parents and children, the relationship between the mother and the father will be disharmonious, and discord will reign among the children. Further, there will be no harmony in one's neighborhood or country. All of the different groups will conflict with each other. There will be discord with one's in-laws, employers and employees will not work well together, and teachers and students will be unable to get along. Therefore, I must cut off all of your influence upon me. What is the use of holding on to reifying habits? As Candrakīrti wrote in his *Autocommentary to the Middle Way*, "I contend that one must completely overcome the tendency to reify one's thinking."

4 The Reifying Habit Compares Its Benefits with Those that Wisdom Offers

The reifying habit replies:

Just telling me to go away, without cultivating an effective meditative practice, is a fruitless course to follow. Without a remedy that is actually effective at directly combating my habits of conceiving the world, even if the united forces of the Buddha, dharma, and sangha should rise up against the principal adversaries of all beings, adorn themselves with armor, and employ an arsenal of numerous sharp weapons that have remarkable powers to shoot, slay, and expel these adversaries, most everything they would do would in the end reinforce my resources, as we have just observed. Wisdom, no matter what you attempt, you are left to bewail, "Go away," "Get out!" but you are unable to lay siege to me. Hence, we do not need to discuss the pathetic potential of ordinary sentient beings who have come under my sway. And you are trying to convince me that your prowess includes obtaining liberation!

Most of the great philosophical and tantric meditators can be recognized by the way they go on mouthing their incantations, during which it is said they generate some clairvoyance; but in their hearts they remain my disciples, and they pay attention mainly to me. They perform an assortment of activities on behalf of various worldly interests, and they have the distinction of being very learned from studying many texts, ascetic from having received and practiced tantric initiations, and good-hearted from having long practiced proper cultivation; nevertheless, if they had to choose between wisdom and myself, the majority of them would still choose me. And why is that? You have neither food nor clothing to give them, nor do you offer good things of any kind. It is even doubtful to them whether you'll be available in the next life!

On the other hand, I am able to provide them with everything they need for the present: tea, alcohol, a good deal of high quality food, a degree of honor and respectful homage that they will earn by being a practitioner, including the value and utility of all the offerings that people will bring them, etc. All that they now enjoy is due to me. Everything that was planted, along with all the results of the harvest, was mostly my doing. I provide people with every requisite for making them happy and bringing them joy. Yes, I'm the one who keeps tying them down with the tight bonds of the eight abiding worldly concerns,[1] while during these times you have always been missing-in-action. Presently, I enable folks to amass every requirement—high, low, and in-between—while you always arrive late with not much more than a few slogans.

So you listen to me, wisdom: people have serious doubts about you. Although everyday existence may be flawed, there is no indication that these practitioners have any confidence in you since they are ready to sell the dharma for the good of their bellies. Monks readily abandon the yards where the scholarly debates are held and wander off to the attractions of the city; they abandon their vows and entertain women; they desert right conduct and concentrate on accomplishing their desires; and they forsake the quiet of remote hermitages in favor of places where they can make a disturbing commotion like a pack of dogs. Instead of renouncing desire, they renounce modesty; instead of renouncing cyclic existence, they renounce liberation; instead of renouncing the eight abiding worldly concerns, they renounce concentrating the mind; instead of renouncing me, they renounce emptiness! They sell important tantric initiations for some new clothes. They may take vows, but only so that they can better market Buddhism. They perform funerary services with one eye kept on the profit they will make, polluting both this life and the next one for a trifle. And so forth—if I really cared to, I could augment this long list endlessly. Each and every one of these futile activities is my own good work, which I accomplished while you were nowhere to be seen. So please stop all of your whining about me being the one who must depart.

Kindly listen to this, wisdom. Although the name "dharma" is used widely, it is merely a label. If one fails to continuously recall death's significance, how can the basis for satisfactory subsequent lifetimes be prepared? Even when one contemplates seriously the many general and particular shortcomings of our cyclic existence and takes them to heart, visualizing them carefully, if one does not develop a mind that wishes to be liberated it is impossible to obtain even the elementary liberation of the Hearer disciples. And when one is unable to develop a love for every sentient being with the same overwhelming sincerity of affection that one feels spontaneously for one's only child, or when one is not eager to carry other people's burdens and willingly assist them with their sufferings, then it is *not* to be expected that one will be able to develop that high aspiration that characterizes a Great Vehicle practitioner.

Only when one has come to depend upon a steady diet of continuous calm-abiding can the wisdom that combats my mode of conceiving things be cultivated properly. Wisdom, if your kind of meditation, which involves analyses that are directed to an investigation of the preeminent modes of being, is not guided by intensive study and meditative practice, then a genuine cultivation of the highest insight will remain out of reach. Therefore, please don't tell *me* to go away! Although you keep crying, "Go away," "Get out!" I have been the close companion of the mind throughout many previous lifetimes, so the mind and I are already accustomed to being each other's intimate companions. No one knows where you might have been keeping yourself during all of this time, so please don't think you can just show up here and take my place. And still you press on!

Those who have attained the level of master practitioners in the past are as rare as the Giant Lotus; and there may be a select few who have been able to accomplish what you are asking. Some people like to call me "ignorance" and make the claim that as soon as one awakens from this ignorance "buddhahood" can be attained. However, I was the mind's friend long before you ever were. I have in my retinue no less than 84,000 emotional afflictions,[2] for which there is said to be 84,000 antidotes. Though you may claim that you have just as many antidotes, no one is able to recognize them well enough to count them; moreover, the ability to properly link which antidote goes with which emotional affliction is out of reach entirely. If you are unable to sort out the antidotes correctly, then you will be unable to overcome even a single one of my much longed for emotional afflictions. Therefore, the notion of your overcoming *all* of them gives me one more occasion for a hearty laugh!

---

[1] Seeking possessions, fearing any loss of possessions, desire for fame, the wish to avoid becoming unpopular, seeking praise, wanting to avoid criticism, savoring pleasure, and avoiding misery.

[2] The 84,000 emotional afflictions may be subdivided into 21,000 types of attachment, 21,000 kinds of anger, 21,000 varieties of ignorance, and 21,000 types that are combinations of the aforementioned three.

5 Wisdom's Soliloquy

Wisdom offers a defense:

My goodness, you have delivered such a fine speech! However, with a little capsicum on his tongue, even a son who has killed his father can be made articulate. What you say is complete falsehood. When it is viewed from the ultimate perspective of perfect wisdom it is only a variety of the ordinary common sense that keeps obscuring things. From the thickets of this obscurantism you have observed a great many things, but they are mostly a mass of contradictions. You offer the confused hubbub of the streets where people tirelessly blather nonsense. In fact, you have not presented a single sound proposition, and the way that you go on is senseless; however, you do provide an excellent display that may make it easier for people to recognize the very sorts of thinking they need to avoid.

If you are receptive to some reliable reasoning, I will now summarize your contradictions for you. You rely upon an assortment of concepts that are burdened by mental afflictions. Fortunately, in the light of ultimate reality these concepts will eventually disappear. All brooks make a great clamor, but an ocean sometimes barely announces itself. And like the ocean, the Buddha spoke a great truth quietly, without uttering anything false. Your many falsehoods could be specified one by one, yet the principal falsehood is the idea that things bear their own true existence—they do not! Even the truth lacks a true nature of its own.

You said that from the beginning you have always abided with the mind, but tell me, is this mind really so permanent, or is it actually impermanent? If you say the mind is permanent, that would render all causal production impossible. And if you say there is no causal production, then your argument that you can influence the mind can be dismissed directly. If, on the other hand, you believe that the mind is impermanent, then what I want to know is did you exist with the mind during a previous instant, during a subsequent instant, or during a moment that is neither of them? If you say that you existed with the mind during the previous instant, then you have accepted something that contradicts your own position, since for you the mind of that previous instant has a mode of appearing that exists inherently; consequently, that mind you are living with would be unable to experience even that much change. And if that is the situation, ignorance could never be remedied: ignorance could not transform itself into any other nature, it would be permanently stable, and it would endure forever! It would even be unable to transform into a subsequent moment, which would then rule out its ability to exist further, even in the present. Anything that is established as truly existing in-itself is incapable of changing, pure and simple; and anything that changes cannot have an existence that is inherently true. This is how it is.

If you accept that you coexist with the mind during a subsequent instant, the mind will somehow have to transform itself so that it will be able to arise in that future moment. Just how is it going to do that? Such coming-to-arise is a phenomenon of production, and you have ruled out all change and production. Moreover, anything labeled "subsequent instant" is subsequent only in dependence upon there being a "previous instant." Only given an interdependence of relations can one reasonably posit such production, and being "truly established" with an essence that is inherent allows no scope for that sort of dependency! There is no production without change. And the idea that a perpetually stable permanence can have any relations with something that is other is ignorant thinking, is it not? This notion is self-contradictory.

Or can it be that you reside with the mind in the present? In that case the mind still has to have previous and subsequent moments, so the same logical difficulties that we just examined—of inherently true being not permitting such change—will reappear. That is, you cannot be abiding with the mind in an inherent present, since a present requires for its existence both previous and subsequent moments, which as we have seen are impermissible according to any notion of truly inherent being. When we analyze the present not only generally speaking but examine the smallest possible instant of it during which something can take place,[1] when we reach the very end of such a present instant there will no longer be room enough for you and the mind to dwell together! If at the end of that brief time there is no longer anything that can be perceived, with whom is it that you will be abiding? What will have become of your truly established inherent being that never changes into anything else? Don't you see how ludicrous your position is and how everything that you believe involves some patent contradiction?

You are responsible for generating the three poisons.[2] Whenever you generate anger, the first poison, for you the anger seems to possess an inherent being of its very own. When it appears to have such an enduring being, the possibility of its being transformed into any other nature is rendered unlikely. Therefore, it appears that you may be stuck with that anger forever! Your position would rule out even its being transformed into greed. And should any greed come to be generated, according to you it too would be unable to transform itself into anything else; that is, if it has a truly existing stable permanence and endures forever, it would be impossible for it to transform itself into anything other than the unchanging, permanent greed that it appears to be. For instance, there is no way that it could become ignorance or any closed-mindedness like that. If you want to claim that you abide together with ignorance too, then the same faults would apply there that arose in the case of your dwelling together with the anger and greed, and you will quickly run out of places to live.

You keep claiming that you have always and only lived alongside the mind, but a truly existing mind such as the one that you imagine is unable to transform itself into anything else, does not depend upon anything besides itself, is permanent and endures forever. Such a mind would be incompatible even with its own varying retinue of 51 secondary mental factors, and it would have to exist independently of all of them, which is more contradictory nonsense. That would mean that the mind's retinue of 51 secondary mental factors would have to exist without having a place where they could base themselves.

Although there are indeed 84,000 mental afflictions as you suggest, if the mind has the stable, inherent existence that you claim it has, it would be incapable of generating all of those afflictions. It could not hold onto any virtues, non-virtues, nor attributes whose moral character is unspecified, since an unchanging mind would be unable to provide scope for any of them. If the mind has an established nature that is inherent, then virtue, vice and so forth, karma and its consequences—including any new accumulations of propensities, and the experiences that they provoke—cannot occur. There could not be the endlessly repetitive cycles of destructive behavior, the lasting peace of reconciliation,[3] nor the 84,000 antidotes to mental delusions taught by the Buddha. Also, there would not be the home of refuge in the three jewels,[4] nor the three poisons and everything that the three poisons generate, including the 84,000 mental afflictions. In short, nothing could exist, which would leave you with nothing more than a heap of contradictions. Don't you see that if the mind has the sort of absolute existence you imagine it has, all of the things that you claimed to be part of your retinue, including all of those 84,000 mental afflictions to which you say you have given your blessings, would be rendered impossible? You are just like a blind person who keeps trying to stare.

Why do you make all these insane accusations? No phenomenon is truly established, and the establishment of inherent being would prevent anything from existing. If there have never been any cycles of changing existence, the mind would be unable to spend lifetimes in the realms of the gods, or in the formless realms, and one would always be stuck with the perspectives of the one same mind with which you say it is that you have always been abiding. With the fixations as firmly established as your thesis of truly inherent being would propose, a mind would be incapable of transforming itself into anything, and it could never be reborn somewhere else. When later one finds oneself born in one of the lower realms, the experiential constituents of living being[5] would themselves belie any inherent existence. During fortunate rebirths, such as those of a god and so forth, the objects that are perceived by the senses similarly appear to be truly established with an inherent being of their own, and they can appear as if they always possessed this being, i.e., as if they did exist without depending upon anything else and were unchangeable and permanent. But if that were really so, then how would it be possible for such beings to ever die or to migrate to a subsequent life? If you say that death and migration to the next life are still possible, it would have to happen completely autochthonously or else it would be inconsistent with that truly established being that is unable to undergo any change. For instance, if the body of a goddess truly had an inherent being, the body could never die, or be reborn.

When all of the five aspects of desire (form, sound, smell, taste, and touch) apprehend the figure of a beautiful goddess, one can become fixated upon what is thought to be the truly inherent being of the beauty of the figure that is perceived. If that figure truly exists in the way you think it does, it should always endure without undergoing any change. So what purpose is served by one's attachments to the other four sources of sensual desire, i.e. the goddess' voice, scent, etc.? Any multiple production of truly existing sensory attachments like this would be superfluous, and they might impinge upon the ontological independence of the inherent being of the beauty of the goddess's figure.

The concretization of a goddess's beauty like this can lead to sentiments of love, which is something else that mistakenly appears to be independently existing and truly established with inherent being. Of course, any inherent phenomenon like that would be unable to change its character, so once such a sincere, truly existing love has been established there could be no quarreling such as those of the demigods, and they would be unable to generate the anger that demigods normally do. If they did, it would directly contradict the thesis that love is absolute; that is, any generation of anger would contradict the purported independent existence of a truly existing love. Demigods are prone to generate vicious anger, and when they do, their anger also is concretized and appears to them to exist inherently. When their battles have finally ended and they return home, they may again try to show some affection, but in the face of an inherently existing anger any attractive aspects will be left unappreciated; otherwise, if they were appreciated, the inherent being of their anger would be undermined. If you say that the attractiveness is simply generated anew, such attraction would not have an inherent essence.

If you insist that there must necessarily be inherent existence, then nothing will be capable of living up to your expectations. If a single mind had inherent being, nothing could affect it. For it, no phenomenon could function, and everything that results merely from the projections of customary reflection would be unable to sustain its existence. In short, we would have to conclude that nothing really exists at all because things do not live up to your belief that for phenomena to really exist they must have true, inherent being, exist in themselves without dependence upon any outside factors, and must necessarily be established by their own essences in just the way that they appear.

On the contrary, all everyday phenomena exist only by virtue of locally contingent conventions and are mutually dependent with their causes and conditions. Somehow, concepts and names have come to be applied to them, and their existence is nothing more than this. If there existed a single, entirely independent phenomenon, it would be impossible for a second phenomenon to engage it. The very nature of an inherently true being would rule out its being a phenomenon that depends upon conditions for its existence; but if this is ruled out, there could not be any phenomena at all.

My own perspective is that phenomena arise due to causes and conditions, with which they are interconnectedly dependent. For me, all phenomena are able to exist this way, and one can experience both karma and its results. The stages of a bodhisattva's evolution exist, as well as the path of evolution and the three jewels. Nevertheless, the being of every entity is admixed with many contingent conventions; that is, things have merely a conventional existence. If one demands that every object must have inherent being, then we will be forced to conclude that none of them really exists.

From the obscurity of your ignorance you behold everything to exist inherently. Further, this causes you to overlook the actual conventional existence of phenomena and therefore deny *that* existence, which is an ignorance that transcends ignorance itself. Yours is a great swirling cyclone of ignorance! Although you mouth the claim that your views are in accord with those of ordinary common sense, all conventional things are established in dependence upon causes and conditions. But you accept the position that things must have *independent* being, so for you mundane phenomena cannot exist. In fact, for you death can never occur; likewise, nothing can be born.

Take the case of when you were a goddess who was reborn as a demigod. When you perceived your physical and mental components as a goddess, you reified those aspects as truly existing and incapable of transforming. Perhaps you thought, "Oh, this is me!" while you were fixating upon your self as a goddess. And then, after you became a demigod,. you similarly fixated upon *that* body, again thinking, "Oh, this is me!" How can it be that these two inherent beings abide alongside each other on a single and still inherent basis? Did the goddess with the splendid aura suddenly begin to go around engaging in competitive jealousies? Wasn't that splendid aura, and that scent, which was inseparable from you while you were a goddess, supposed to have an invariable, inherent essence? Did that jealous and competitive mind come to inhabit your inherent nature all by itself?

It is inconceivable that an inherently existing and unchangeable essence of a goddess and an inherently existing and unchangeable essence of a demigod could cohabit the same self. If you contend that after the goddess, which was established as having inherent being, perishes, the demigod replaces her and also has inherent being, it would follow that something that has inherent essence is able to transform itself into something else whenever required; in other words, birth and death do not really have inherent being. Should something with inherent being transform itself into something else that has inherent being, your position that things do not change would be contradicted.

If things existed inherently in the way you claim they do, transmigration would be impossible. When you are reborn as a hungry ghost, for instance, the terrific suffering of hunger and thirst that the hungry ghost experiences would have to be accompanied by that previous splendid goddess's aura of yours, since it was permanent, unchanging, and forever enduring. And with all of the meals that a goddess gets to eat, it is unlikely that you ever would become hungry, despite your being a hungry ghost. Having consumed so many bellyfuls of food, you will always feel satiated—a satiation that you must think is incapable of changing—so how is it that you suddenly have become so hungry?! If you are a hungry ghost who truly exists, it is your body's essence to always be hungry and thirsty. If that hunger and thirst are really part of your inherent nature, they will be unable to transform themselves into any other condition, even after you are reborn. In fact, it seems quite likely that one day you will grow feint and collapse from that sort of constant hunger.

Once you are reborn in hell, the newly experienced suffering from the fires and freezing encountered there would surely disabuse you of the nonsense that there could be no rebirth. The act of rebirth itself will undermine the possibility of existing by virtue of an inherent essence. Once you begin to experience the sufferings of the terrible heat of hell, to where do you think the joy and pleasures of the goddess could have disappeared? How do you think it is possible that the supposedly changeless and independent happiness of the godly realm—which was supposed to exist on its own basis and to be ever incapable of changing into another nature—has turned into painful suffering from pervasive heat? Since happiness and suffering are mutually contradictory and each has inherent existence, how is it possible that they could coexist in one self? When you are about to transmigrate from your lifetime as a goddess, the great bliss of that time should be incapable of transforming itself into any other nature. If the goddess's bliss had its own essence, it would be unchangeable and could never transform into the suffering of the hot hells, which would have to have an unchanging, inherent essence of its own. Despite the fact that these two essences cannot coexist, you're still very pleased with your notion that both of them exist by virtue of having an inherent existence, aren't you?

How is it that you are so very confident that this faulty notion of inherent being has absolute qualities that you are determined to hold onto it no matter what? If the terrible suffering that one experiences in the cold hells and the suffering that one endures in the hot hells both had inherent essences, they could never be transformed into one another, even for an instant. And yet, just as if these two sufferings maintained a close friendship, the inherent essence of the suffering of cold—which you insist must be permanent and eternal—would have to accompany the suffering from heat, as if one of them was piled right on top of the other. But hot and cold are mutually contradictory, and so their two inherent essences must also be completely contradictory. How could these two sufferings function in such proximity to each other? How would they manage to coexist in the same self while still retaining their inherent nature?

Despite all of these evident and pervasive contradictions, you remain satisfied with your notion of inherent existence, do you not? Nevertheless, the notion that the existence of things is due to their own inherent essences is mistaken. When someone is about to obtain a human body, you must think that one acquires that body out of the sheer blue, since according to you there can be no rebirth. How strange it is that you deny your own rebirth—you are the very epitome of ignorance.

Through endless cycles of rebirths, a sentient being keeps taking rebirth in one or another of the various realms, and you wish to concretize an inherent existence for each and every one of them, based upon a reification of the principal experiential and physical aspects of its being.[6] Each of these conceived aspects is reified in the very way it has come to be concretized in one's thinking. These conceptually fixed aspects of being seem to be independent, changeless, and dependent upon nothing outside of themselves in precisely the ways that one has come to determine them; and one imagines that they cannot be transformed further, beyond what one has just framed! What is simply a fortuitous coherence of the constituents of one's being that presents itself is made the basis for thinking, "I am," and this idea is grasped obsessively, and then contrived to be existing truly in-itself just in the way that it has happened to appear.

According to you, a sentient being has a distinctly separate body for each lifetime of residence in any of the six realms.[7] If this is so, by what procedure are all of these bodies able to assemble together in one entity with their inherent essences? Maybe your thinking is confused, because how could all of them possibly reside together in harmony? Each of the beings that dwell in the six realms have their own unique experiences, which can include unbearable sufferings that may be mutually exclusive of each other, such as extreme heat and extreme cold. If each one of these sufferings possesses an inherent essence that is independent, in need of nothing besides itself, changeless, permanent, and always persisting, then all of them would necessarily have to be experienced by you now together, and *at the same time*. But how can that be possible? Even if your body did experience them that way, it would only demonstrate the untruth of your contention that their inherent essences never change. So long as their nature exists inherently, it is impossible for all of these contradictory experiences to coexist harmoniously on the same basis.

What is simply a fortuitous coherence of aspects of your being that presents itself is given the concept 'I,' which is concretized and then perceived to exist on its own. *This notion too is reified as something that has its own inherent essence.* This is how the apprehension of the self of a person arises. When one focuses obsessively upon that self, the idea of a person becomes fixed; when it is reified in this way, the notion of inherent existence is established. Thinking like this arises very naturally in the mind: an 'I' is concretized on the basis of the physical, emotional and mental aspects of a person's being, and that 'I' appears to exist by virtue of its own essence, in the very way that it serendipitously came to be witnessed.

It is necessary to identify flawlessly the object that is to be negated and to refute it by using formal analysis. One does not merely refute an 'I'; rather, one must capture *precisely* the very mode by which one has infused that object with permanence, etc., and make *this* the principal object of negation. In fact, that is our main enemy. Nevertheless, you persist in holding a host of obviously erroneous positions about these aspects of being, which I am happy to outline for you.

Consider this question: do (1) that which has become the 'I,' and (2) the aggregated aspects of being upon which the 'I' is based, exist on their own as one *identical* being, or do they exist as two fundamentally *different* entities? If you say it is one identical being, then it must exist entirely without difference: it must not change into anything that has a different nature, it cannot depend upon anything other than itself, and it must be independent, changeless, and so exist perpetually. If that is hcw it is, when one dies and one's body is burned and one's ashes are tossed in the air or into the river, would those aspects of being (which according to you would be incapable of changing) become completely non-existent? Not only that, would the 'I' also become non-existent at that time? It would, would it not, since it is unable to transform itself? If the collected aspects of being are established as existing truly from their own side, to where do you think they might have gone? On the other hand, if the 'I' and the components of one's being are *transformed* in taking another rebirth, it would indeed be a very peculiar sort of changelessness that these aspects would have according to your account, i.e., a changelessness that keeps changing through various rebirths.

If the components of being are innately changeless and must always remain just as they are according to their inherent essence, then why was the term "dying" ever even devised? Moreover, if there can be no dying, there can be no being born; and if there is no being born, how could illness, old age, etc. ever occur? Maybe for you nothing exists at all. On the other hand, if birth and death do exist, they cannot have inherent essence. According to your way of thinking, phenomena are supposed to exist without change or any dependence upon other factors. You deny that the existence of any phenomenon is established and sustained by virtue of its mutual relations with other phenomena; therefore, for you no phenomena can exist! Yet you keep saying that things are changeless and incapable of transforming themselves into anything else. You are the perfect model of delusion; and amidst so much self-delusion you are ignorant even of your own ignorance.

When you are reborn in other realms, for you the collected aspects of your being and the 'I' must exist as a single entity that has an inherent essence. Having concretized this fortuitous coherence of aspects of your being this way, you will need to be able to proceed to other rebirths that have their own aspects of being, such as rebirths as animals, with that identical notion 'I' in tact. Moreover, you will need to keep carrying those various non-human aspects of being with you, as inherent to your identity! Since it would be directly contradictory for the human and non-human aspects to abide together, this is nonsense.

Debating with you is like debating with someone who is deranged, especially since nothing I say has any effect upon you. It is like debating with a stone. In fact, you are worse than a stone; at least a stone can be sculpted, and its shape will respond to what the sculptor does, but you have an ignorance that remains oblivious to everything. You don't even accept death! When you die and take another birth, if after that rebirth the aspects of your previous being remain absolute, can never be separated from you, and keep abiding, then please explain to me what is the function of dying?

If you carry with you to your next birth whatever aspects of being you have become accustomed to, then how can the being that is conceived in a subsequent mother's womb have any true existence of its own, in the way you want to speak of it? And how do you manage to retain the identical aspects of being throughout all of these various lives? If you claim that you hold on to them in spite of these changes, the phenomenon of change itself betrays your assertion that your inherent existence never changes. Any rebirth that has its aspects of being already established is itself contrary to the idea of inherent existence.

If 'I' and the aspects of being exist as a single entity, you will be unable to reify the conceived object "mine" as something that exists in itself, since if mineness exists inherently it would have to be something that exists *separately* from the 'I.'[8] If you do reify the concept "mine," when you and your aspects of being change, as happens during death and rebirth, it would render untenable the notion that this "mine" has an inherent essence that undergoes no change. For instance, when one conceives the idea "my hand," this mineness can seem to possess an inherent essence, which does not change and is permanent, independent, and relies upon nothing other than itself. It seems to exist by virtue of its own inherent nature as something that will never change; however, when this same "mineness" of my hand is made part of the notion of my foot, etc., these subsequent reifications of mineness undermine the contention that mineness is unchanging.

If you persist in thinking that mineness has an inherent essence, then consider the fact that anything that exists in itself without ever changing cannot keep turning into things that have different inherent essences. You are unable to defend your essentialism any longer. You may become attached to notions that you have concretized as things that have inherent essences, but sometimes they will not fulfill your expectation that their attractiveness is perpetual and unchanging, in the way you have conceived them. For example, when you see a woman to whose form your eyes have become attached, her attractiveness gets concretized and her beauty seems to really exist on its own; however, the permanent, inherent quality of this attachment is proven false as soon as you generate new attachments, which seem to have similarly permanent, inherent existence. As soon as a new attachment is generated, the status of the prior attachment as always enduring is lost, and the notion that those attachments are inherently real *in themselves* is proven to be illusory.

Similarly, the conceptual objects that are concretized by each one of the other senses appear to have their inherent natures, to which one becomes attached, but these are also false conceptions. Each newly generated attachment further undermines the notion that these attachments are invariable and have inherent essences. From the very first instant that an object appears to our sight, it is seized upon as existing independently and thought to have an inherent essence, to which we become obsessively attached. We think that these objects and our attachments to them truly exist in the very way that we have conceived them. The aspects of our being that we have just examined were also thought to exist on their own from the very beginning; however, we learned that if they did exist that way, there could be no rebirth in the other five realms of existence. Beliefs like those have no validity.

The transitory nature of our present human form contradicts any contention that such being has existed this way from time immemorial. For example, do you seriously think that the progression from infancy to old age leads to an independently existing elderly body that existed in the beginning just the way it exists now? Even discounting for your ignorance, this remains a notion that one can laugh at. How it is possible that from the moment a mother has given birth until a person has reached old age, there has been no change at any point, and that both the infant and the elder have always existed inherently this way? Please explain to me, how did this old man find his way into the mother's womb?

Why is it necessary to generate in your mind an obsessive attachment to each one of the five constituents of sentient being, since there is already an unchangeable truly existing attachment to the reified 'I,' and the 'I' and the constituents of sentient being are supposed to be truly existing as one identical entity? If you did generate these new attachments, it would contradict the notion that nothing is produced anew. If we were to apply this kind of reasoning to all of your thinking and to all of your attachments, there would be no end to the work that we would face.

If you argue instead that the 'I' and the constituents of sentient being have inherent existence as *different* entities, two objects that are truly different should have no connections with each other; accordingly, when one's hand is hurt and you say "I hurt," no mineness should be operative between the hand and the 'I' because they would each exist inherently as entirely separate entities.

My head and my mouth would similarly exist separately from each other, and so would the tip of my nose, my sight and the other sense powers; *my* body, *my* stomach, *my* hip, *my* knee, *my* hunger, *my* thirst, clothing, etc.; *my* farm, *my* house, *my* servant, *my* wife, *my* children, etc.; and all of my possessions including the aspects of my sentient being have somehow all crystallized as phenomena that are "mine." In each case the mineness has been reified to such an extent that it appears to exist inherently on its own as a phenomenon that is completely different from my mind and with which it cannot have a relationship, even though it is the mind that has generated it! Incredibly, these phenomena that are "mine" appear to have their own inherently separate essences, and they seem to exist without any relations with the 'I' that gave them birth. Trying to figure out how a truly existent 'I' and a truly existent "mine" can each exist independently of the other must lead you to exhaustion. The reification of truth habits (according to which entities appear to possess their being as inherent essences) and wisdom itself are incompatible and unable to coexist in the same place.

There is no sense to the idea that a "mine" could be fixed to one of the constituents of sentient being that has already been conceived and concretized as existing inherently separate from the 'I.' Since the inherent "mine" can have no relations with them, the possibility that these independent constituents can be "mine" must be excluded. Accordingly, mineness cannot come into force without contradicting your ludicrous position. You are mistaken, but you still wish to have minenesses that are independent, despite the fact that there is no reason to support you; therefore, if you were to just keep silent, it would please everyone.

If the 'I' and the constituents of sentient being exist as multiple phenomena, each with its own inherent essence, then it follows that the 'I' and the constituents of a person must also be phenomena that exist inherently as one, for the reason stated in Nāgārjuna's *Jeweled Rosary*[9]: "Without existing as one, there cannot be an existing as many." Accordingly, if you accept that something exists as many, it must also exist as one. So if you insist upon arguing, "It follows that the 'I' and the constituents of my sentient being are one because the 'I' and the constituents exist by virtue of one single inherent essence," that would contradict what is explained in Candrakīrti's *Entering the Middle Way*[10]: if the 'I' and the constituents of sentient being existed inherently as one, each one of the parts of these constituents of sentient being would have to exist inherently as one, and so the 'I' would become multiple; therefore, it could not be one.

Similarly, each of the parts into which the cardinal directions are divided—east, west, north, south, and center—would also have inherent individuality. Taking the case of the center position as a model, although it may be one, it too would have to have eastern, western, central, etc. portions. Likewise, when the smallest possible particle —even a tiny speck of iron—is split into parts, you would still want to hold on to the idea that each individual sub-speck exists by virtue of its own inherent essence, right up to the point where not even any dust remains. How can all of those tiny specks manage to remain together as an inherently existing single entity, when according to you these miniscule parts must also bear their own tiny individual true essences. If the 'I' and each of the constituents of sentient being exist by virtue of their own individual inherent nature in this way, and those essences never change, when you keep dividing their parts into ever smaller inherently existing individual particles, at the end of this to where do you think your inflated 'I' with its inherent essence will have disappeared?

Though the 'I' and the components of sentient being continuously keep changing, you claim that they never change. This must be the reason why their inherent existence is so amazingly special!

---

[1] According to Tibetan folklore, this is said to be 1/60th of a finger snap.

[2] Anger, greed and ignorance.

[3] *Myong 'das* (*nirvana*).

[4] The three jewels are the Buddha, the doctrine (Dharma), and the spiritual community (Saṃgha).

[5] *Phung po*, the physical, emotional, and mental constituents of a person. The reference is to the five "aggregated" factors, i.e. form and various aspects of conceptual and emotional being, which according to Buddhist metaphysics compose the existence of a person. This notion "aspects of being" or "constituents of being" plays a vital role in Buddhist thinking.

[6] *Phung po*; see preceding footnote.

[7] The six realms are the realms of the gods, demigods, humans, animals, hungry ghosts, and hell beings.

[8] At this point, Khenpo Lobsang Tsering remarked, "There are a great many reasonings that are implicated here." One of them is that any possession must involve at least two entities, as in "my form," "my perception," etc. The principal point is that these must involve duality, which rules out the option that inherent existence can occur as a single, self-sufficient entity.

[9] A paraphrase of *Rin po che'i phreng ba* (*Ratnavali*), stanza 85.

[10] *Dbu ma la 'jug pa* (Madhyamakāvatāra); stanza 127.

6 The Reifying Habit Satirizes Practitioners

The one who is obsessed with truth habits replies:

No matter how long you go on with your loud blathering, no one is impressed, and your words do not frighten me. You might as well be presenting your explanations of dharma to a boulder, which cannot be moved no matter how much you agitate it. You will only end up with a case of dry-mouth! Although you expect that one day your fine teachings will lead folks to having interested attention, there is not much chance of that. And if you wish to know why, I can explain it to you.

Those beings who live as gods are always distracted by their many careless preoccupations, while demigods are given to being distracted by their petty jealousies. Animals and brute beings are preoccupied by the tasks of chasing each other or avoiding being eaten. Beings that live as hungry ghosts are distracted by their interminable hunger and poverty. Beings who live in hells are distracted by their sufferings from the heat or the cold. Some humans are continuously distracted by the efforts required for killing; others are distracted by the work of thieving. Some humans are distracted by the acrimony of divisive talk; others are distracted by their own pretense to having an intimate knowledge of Buddhist doctrine.

Some humans are distracted by their attempts to simulate profound meditation; others are distracted by their efforts to market a simulation of the dharma. Some humans are distracted by their efforts to deceive the faithful; others are distracted by profitable agricultural pursuits or by other commercial interests. Some humans are distracted by the allure of sexual entanglements; others are distracted by their habituation to intoxicants. Some humans are distracted by their desire to sleep or by laziness; others are distracted by their engaging in constant idle chatter. Some humans are distracted by their work projects, industrious diversions, creative pursuits, or by recreational activities, including gambling; others spend their time abiding in a thoughtless daze. All of them are distracted by being stuck inside of the ruts of their own bewildered thinking! A few humans are distracted by the consequences of having committed horrible deeds that bear karmic influences that are not easily removed; and most people are distracted by one or more of the ten non-virtuous actions,[1] of which you have spoken. They live without much purpose and will be unable to appreciate whatever you try to tell them.

Even most great meditators have not learned the dharma very well, so when you offer them your fine reasoning, they will be unable to understand much of what you are saying. Scholars who have engaged themselves in their studies think a great deal of their knowledge, even though they never engage in any practice; accordingly, these wise ones will not have much respect for your advice either. They spend so much time searching for the faults of others and sorting through all their texts that they have no opportunity to cultivate their own tantric practice. Even those who do get the opportunity to meditate cannot at the time of meditating remember anything of what they have learned. Some may consult a yogi who appears to be a great meditator but knows nothing and only invents some fabulous visualization. I'm forced to laugh out loud once again!

Your destiny is to become very disheartened, and finally you will reach the end of your road. There are precious few people whose meditation is able to generate this difficult Great Mudra of yours, whereas my own Great Mudra is easier to accomplish, which is why so many people practice it. One reason is that it does not require any vows or virtues. Although quite a number of men and women take the three kinds of vows,[2] they do not really feel a need for them, and so they fail to keep a close guard over them. Since they do not esteem the capacities of tantric empowerments highly, they ignore their promises and do not even feel the need to maintain the ten virtues.[3] Your practices are like undergarments, which may be worn or not, as one chooses.

Instead of cultivating the Great Mudra, emptiness, and all that, what people think matters most is to wear their hair up high like a crown, display long turquoise necklaces, earrings, conch-shell and colored iron bracelets, a garland of bones, etc. They also wear many tantric implements all over themselves, including a long dagger, sacred insignia, a tiger skin, skull, a trumpet made from human thigh-bone, and so forth. With all of this paraphernalia at hand, they do not feel compelled to specify any particular cognition. Not considering any ideas, they cultivate these peculiar objects as meditative foci, which only increases their sense of possessiveness; so in the end they become masters of my types of meditation!

If I should give three days of instructions, and then people cultivate my practices for only a month, anyone would easily become free! And by meditating upon utter nothingness in this life and in the next, buddhahood will be obtained. These are my splendid practices, which bring quick results, whereas your kinds are less effective. Eventually, all this will make you depressed. You come along only when there has been a limitless accumulation of good merit, which is very rare, whereas I am always abiding close by. It may eat your heart out, but these many defeats will one day cause you to become greatly fatigued. So it really would be best for you yourself if you did not come here anymore.

---

[1] The ten non-virtues are killing, stealing, sexual misconduct, lying, sander, harsh speech, idle gossip, covetousness, malicious intent, and wrong view (see Rigdzin 1986: 203). Four of these are attributable to one's speech, three to one's body, and three to one's mind.

[2] These are the vows of personal emancipation (*prātimokṣa* / Hinayana), universal emancipation (*bodhicitta*/Mahayana), and *tantra* (*mantrayana*).

[3] These are the opposite of the ten non-virtues listed in footnote 1.

7 Wisdom Explains How to Treat Appearances

Wisdom responds with this account of appearance and reality:

All your testimonials to your true existence are mere fits of egotism. You don't possess a single good quality, but your conceit has led you to become convinced that you are informed about everything. Never mind having good qualities, you don't even have friends! You offer vigorous words about your independence and proclaim that you are enduring, unchanging, and permanent, but in reality you are clueless.

Not a single one of your friends subscribes to the logic of your tenets, which asserts that there are no phenomena except yourself. Since I accept all the interconnectedly dependent relations of phenomena, everyone can be my friend. In fact, since all phenomena have mutual dependence, not only am I their friend, they are also dependent upon me; hence, I accompany them necessarily. Further, since phenomena are merely projections, it is critical that I accompany them.

Phenomena are composites that arise by virtue of causes and conditions, and I am one of those conditions. In dependence upon the rising and setting of the sun and moon, we distinguish the day from the night. It is the interdependence of summer, winter, fall, and spring that allow them to occur in just the way they do; similarly, fruits ripen in dependence upon water that is brought by rains. The cycle of work in the fields exists as interdependent activities, as do the births and deaths of living beings, sickness and suffering, hot and cold, hunger and thirst, etc. All of these situations occur adventitiously: based upon certain conditions, some things arise, including eating, sleeping, going, and even remaining in place, and so forth. The body's motions, its extensions and contractions, also can occur. Speech proclaims, and so one listens to what is said; eyes see, and one focuses one's attention, et cetera. Attachment, anger, and ignorance; jealousy, envy and deceit; the 84,000 afflictive emotions, and so on: everything can be witnessed to materialize and vanish in dependence upon incidental conditions. This includes the existence of "earlier" and "later" moments along with the existence of their individuality, as well as the names that are applied to each mutually differentiated individual moment. All of them arise in mutual dependence upon something that is other than themselves.

These causes and conditions generate things that have mutually establishing, interconnectedly dependent being. In just this way, all of them are indeed my intimate companions! Furthermore, I am their friend, too, since if they did not exist, I could not exist; and if I did not exist, neither could they. We exist together as friends always do, and if one of us exists, so does the other; but if either of us did not exist, then both of us would be non-existent, much in the way that one is unable to fly with only one wing or walk with only one leg. Because things are this way, one kindness inevitably leads to an increase of other kindnesses! But since you exist all alone, none of these kindnesses is available to you. That is your retribution for embracing the idea that each entity exists individually by itself in a concrete way, with its own inherent essence.

We need to avoid the idea that things that arise on the basis of their phenomenal appearances must either be objects that are independently true or be completely non-existent. That is, we need to appreciate the fact that recognizing that phenomena lack an existence that possesses *inherent* being eliminates both the extreme of truly independent being and the extreme of utter non-existence.

Nihilism is refuted by recognizing that phenomena do have an existence on the basis of their appearing, an appearing that is empty of any truly existing inherent essences. Here is the thinking: because there are contingent appearances, there is emptiness of true existence; and because there is emptiness of true existence, interconnected, dependent appearances can manifest. All these mutually associated phenomena occur just this way! *Appearance and emptiness thus have an attraction for each other*: each solicits the other, and one cannot claim that either one predominates.

Take, for instance, a person who has what is called "the great compassion." This person has been generating it from time immemorial, and all this while it has been the nature of this compassion to be empty of any inherent essence of its own; its being has depended upon its constant engagement with the contingencies that empower it. By realizing compassion's basic emptiness, one's compassion becomes "the great compassion." Compassion and its emptiness exist by virtue of their mutually determining relationship, and the great compassion can only be generated because there is an emptiness of true existence. Their association is intimate, like two horses who scratch each other's back. Cause and effect exist this way—surely compassion and emptiness must have a causal structure, but here one is unable to determine which is the cause and which is the effect, and it is difficult to set out their precise structure.

In your view, should the inherently true being that you propose be demonstrated to be completely non-existent, everything in the world would become incapable of existing. Your belief in inherently true being makes you like a solitary bachelor who lives alone and has a capacity to be self-sufficient in perpetuity. You exist independently, without relying upon anyone, and think you are unchanging and permanently enduring. Among all of the ways to be clueless, your way is the most clueless of them all—indeed, no cluelessness anywhere in the world is greater than yours! The Victorious One never discussed anyone who is more ignorant than you are. Not below the earth, above the earth, nor upon the earth.

You have huge eyes that keep trying to stare intently, but you remain blind to everything. What a wonder it is! Any arising that bears your idea of an absolute, inherent essence will be incapable of arising; consequently, you must deny arising altogether. Similarly, although you witness aging, for you there can be no aging in the way that aging actually occurs; any aging that is absolute would be incapable of getting any older. And any cessation that is absolute will be unable to finally cease. It is your ignorant view that any matters that do not have inherent being will not be able to exist at all; therefore, although illness inflicts harm, people die, and death and cessation occur, you will be compelled by your reasoning to deny the contingent being that all of these phenomena manifest.

If the body's actions existed inherently, it could not act spontaneously. For instance, if either the extension or contraction of the limbs were inherent, the arms and legs could no longer flex or stretch themselves. If there were an inherent going, people could not go in the way that they do; if there were only staying, staying would be unrecognizable. If lying down had inherent essence, there would be no going to lie down. If "sleeping" had inherent being, no one could go to sleep; if "waking up" was inherent, there could be no waking up. If people were always dressing themselves, they would never finish with getting dressed. If any one among seeing, hearing, smelling, tasting, and touching became a permanent activity, the others could never occur. There is no end to the applications of this reasoning. In brief, each phenomenon occurs adventitiously, in dependence upon causes and conditions and the mutually determinative interconnected relations of agents and their actions. An inherent seeing could never change what it is looking at, so it would be lunacy.

Your view is crazier than crazy, but I am probably even crazier to be having this debate with you! Nevertheless, you are an enemy who is never very far away, so I do not have the option of not debating with you. Please don't flatter yourself that we'll ever be anything other than staunch enemies who must debate this way, even though I, wisdom, am indeed tiring of it.

The beings of all the six realms—humans, animals, etc. —are like boulders in that they have extremely stubborn truth habits whose rigidity prevents them from understanding what it is I'm saying, so my advice has no effect. If one meditates upon the nature of the 'I' without wisdom and diligent effort, then no matter what I may say, when my discourse concludes one will be left sitting in an indolent silence. Alas, *sentient beings are always victims of the force of their own habits of thinking*!

They generate the notion of "this mountain" in relation to there being "that mountain." And when they go to "that mountain," previously thought to be "that mountain" because of its interdependence with the previous "this mountain," the identities of the two mountains get reversed, and "that mountain" becomes "this mountain," while the previous "this mountain" becomes "that mountain." In this way we are able to appreciate that the identities we construct are based upon appearances of things that are empty in themselves. An appearance that seems to have true existence does not really exist that way; its being only seems to exist that way, based upon the contingent appearances that were produced.

When we regard the perceptual field, we should refute what seems to be produced and recognize that what arises there has no intrinsic nature of its own and only appears to have one. Candrakīrti tells us that customary truth is the means by which ultimate truth is ascertained. That is, without having a basis of customary conventions to examine, we will be unable to understand the ultimate. *It is from appearances that we discover emptiness.* We should consider this matter very carefully—that emptiness can be fathomed by closely investigating the way that things appear.

In order to appreciate that each and every phenomenon is empty of having an inherent essence of its own, one must also investigate how phenomena that bear names are actually empty of possessing those names as something that is inherent to them; one must investigate how *phenomena develop their sense by having meanings projected upon them,* and how these meanings are constructed by mental conventions, terminological designations, and theoretical elaborations. If one does not analyze them in this way, then all of these phenomena will appear to be real in themselves.

All phenomena appear in conformity with the mere names and notions that get projected upon them, and in this way "cause" and "effect" relations, "actions" and "actors," "birth" and "cessation," etc. arise. Once we ascertain just how we go about creating these "causes," "effects," "actions," and "actors," we will be able to function without taking these imaginary constructions more seriously than they merit. Moreover, understanding emptiness in just this way will simultaneously eliminate nihilistic views. This view of emptiness is gained by deeply ascertaining that "cause" and "effect" exist by virtue of the mere labels and notions that are projected upon events: we reify these identifications of the objects and then fixate upon those reifications. Without exception, all of these reifications need to be destroyed.

Rejecting both the extreme of positivism and the extreme of nihilism, we will generate a precise ascertainment of how action and its results actually occur and begin to think about cause and effect without being deceived. By destroying all these fixations upon our reified identifications of objects, and making an offering of them to all the Victorious Ones, we will come to correctly comprehend the emptiness of what appears; we will recognize the interconnected dependence of appearances, and we will stop being deceived by them. When we generate a precise ascertainment of just how this is, it will become our best offering to the lamas! When we destroy every single reified fixation that we conceive, while ascertaining the exclusively interdependent and occasionally caused phenomena to exist without each having to have their own inherent nature, and then gain some capacity to stabilize that insight, that may be made an offering to the *yidam*-s![1]

When one clearly witnesses the reciprocal being of appearance and emptiness and recognizes the interconnectedly dependent relations of results and causes, it may be made an offering to those beings who dance in the sky! Abiding in the unmistaken witness of the causes and results that pertain to one's own situation, we can also destroy the conceptual objectifications of independent phenomena that are conceived by others. And when we come to see those very clearly, they may be made offerings to the dharma protectors! Having understood the incontrovertible analytic reasoning that pertains to the interdependent relation of causes and effects, one clearly ascertains the emptiness, and that undermines support for any of the reifications constructed by a positivist outlook, which occasionally can cause things to seem to exist independently of anything else. When one obtains a precise understanding that ascertains unmistakably the way that the things that exist are only the contingent effects of their particular causes, it can be made an offering to the great spiritual guardian Shal-zhi-pa![2] By destroying all obsessive attachments to the objects that one's consciousness has reified, one develops a deep understanding that recognizes just how one fixates habitually upon these notions of entities that can seem to have inherent identities.

The obsessive attachments to the objects we conceive in our consciousness become a lifelong continuum of thinking. One must replace that continuum with another one that tenaciously practices the negation of each of those objects. One eliminates only their character of appearing to exist with inherent nature, and one becomes able to sustain continuously a non-affirming negation.[3] This may be made an offering to all of the vajra families.[4]

One needs to establish a calm abiding that has taken emptiness for its object of concentration. The principal instruction for practice is to cultivate penetrating insight, and to abide within an equanimity that cognizes emptiness! Whenever one fails to place oneself in the bliss of a meditative equipoise, one should again thoroughly investigate the nature of things, using the seven ways to formally analyze the lack of inherent essences; otherwise, how will one ever be able to develop penetrating insight? Formal analysis is thus capable of guiding one to a very steady realization. This may then be made an offering to all of the beneficial sponsors of one's practice; may the sponsors and the practitioners pacify their mental continuums together!

---

[1] A *yidam* is the meditative deity that one uses as the focal point for one's meditative absorption.
[2] Shal zhi pa is a guardian of the dharma with four heads and is a meditative deity.
[3] A non-affirming negation is a negation that institutes a thoroughgoing refusal to affirm the existence of any hypostatized entity, and it is contrasted with negations that while negating one thing imply the existence of something else, the classic example being "The fat monk does not eat during the day."
[4] By invoking the vajra families, the Panchen Lama is honoring the tantric practices of all the accomplished Buddhas.

8 The Reifying Habit Rebuts Wisdom

The one who has become addicted to his truth habits describes his own prowess:

O.K. O.K., you have quite a compilation of refutations about me to go on about. But I have a few refutations about you also, so listen carefully! Since you accept that things are established on the basis of dependent relations, your antidote called wisdom is necessarily dependent upon me, the practice that reifies inherent existence. Hence, it is inconsistent for you to assert that *I* am utterly non-existent! If I am non-existent, how will something that is dependent upon me be able to arise? Speaking about the dependent being of something that does not exist is no more reasonable than making assertions about the beauty of the waist of a rabbit who has horns. Or who would ever make a claim, for example, that a coat made of tortoise fur is soft or rough?

The one who has surpassed all victories gave 84,000 collections of teachings that were addressed to my own 84,000 collections of ignorance, of which the three poisons are paramount. One can propose "antidotes" for them, which makes the antidotes dependent upon the ignorance; if the varieties of ignorance did not have existence in the first place, you and your antidotes would be out of business. My logic defeats you!

I am in charge of all these ignorant habits that depend upon mundane conventions and sense, so should I myself come to have no inherent nature, you will be left without any phenomena at all. Because of this contradiction I defeat you!

Why is this? The main practice of the six kinds of beings involves abiding in my ways continuously, where they fall under the sway of the three poisons, which I control along with the ten non-virtues of which the five most heinous crimes[1] are paramount. I spin endlessly the cycles of birth, old age, illness, and death. This includes the important practices of worldly commerce, all of which arise only in dependence upon me! To declare that I don't exist at all is an exaggeration, and it will lead you to nihilism. You are being contradictory! Moreover, you go against what everyday common sense keeps telling us. Contending that my existence does not exist at all is the talk of a blind and crazy person who cries out alone. My logic defeats you!

What actually does not exist for all of the six kinds of beings is wisdom, since there remains colossal work ahead for those meditating upon it before it can come about. You think that things that lack inherent existence still exist somehow, and not infrequently you meditate upon the existence of non-existence! Such a view erroneously succumbs to the distortions of positivism. On the other hand, there is no need for anyone to meditate on me in order for my existence to endure. Whatever it is that one may be seeking can come about through my natural capacity, without anyone having to do any meditation. You meditate upon this nothingness that you have fabricated, but how is a contrived meditation like that going to provide any benefits to anyone? Your practice of a contrived cultivation of the way that things abide and my practice of accepting things the way they actually are stand in direct contradiction with each other.

What you have been trying to argue is completely illogical. What is truly established and what lacks true existence are directly contradictory, and what is dependently established and what is independently established are directly contradictory, just as fabricated phenomena contradict unfabricated phenomena. For this reason the positions you have accepted are irreparably flawed. In the same way that you spoke of how the notion "that mountain" is really established in dependence upon "this mountain," the antidote involving generating this so-called wisdom is dependent upon there being obsessive identifications of entities that have inherently true being; only *after* these latter exist can it become the task of wisdom to negate them. You contradict all of common sense. In sum: if I do not exist, then neither do you!

There must be two people to have a quarrel, and combatting an enemy who doesn't exist is like trying to clap with only one hand. Only when I have being can you contest that being. I may be the one about whom you boast your meditative practice is able to give a whipping, but it is only because I exist that you are able to undertake such work, is that not so? Your attempt by itself contradicts any assertion that I do not exist, and my not existing would render your position untenable.

My afflictions are the starting point for all of your great practices that serve as antidotes for gradually abandoning those afflictions. Are not my afflictions what populate the paths and grounds over which you claim a serious practitioner must proceed? If that is correct, then your attempt to abandon my nature is complicated by the fact that if I do exist, the attempt to abandon me has been unsuccessful; and if I do not exist, there will be nothing for you to abandon.

If we divide up all of the objects of knowledge, then surely more of them will fall under my control than are influenced by you. Despite the considerable egoism that exists everywhere, you still assert, "There is no ego!" It must be that you are either crazy, out of your mind, or not very competent. Egoism is the target that you must aim at when you shoot the arrows of your antidotes. So are you going to shoot or not? If you are, then you require the manifestation of my existence. On the other hand, if you do not shoot, then your arrows will never destroy anything. So you find yourself in a very peculiar predicament. Surely, any practice cultivated by wisdom cannot consist of blindly firing arrows!

The way that wisdom cultivates ideas must differ completely from how I practice conceptualizing matters. For instance, you have been arguing that if something that exists inherently were to transform itself it would contradict the notion that inherent existence never changes, but such a flaw does not apply to me. I have a good argument, so listen to my explanation: each of the afflictive emotions is based strictly upon its own self-establishment, and each one has an inherent being that exists along with each one of them, without it having to depend upon anything else. There is no transformation from being one thing to being another. Whenever an afflictive emotion is being generated, its inherent existence already arrives along with it, so it is not the case that anything is being transformed. Even when the prior instant of an afflictive emotion is about to fade, my habit of reification is operative, and it will still be there with its notions of things existing inherently in-themselves when the succeeding instant begins to appear. This situation holds true equally for all phenomena.

In a large room that is so dark that nothing can be seen, all things will appear black. In that kind of pervading obscurity nothing will be able to transform into anything other than more of the same darkness. That obscurity will saturate every arising and every cessation. In that respect it is a lot like me, and there is no denying the fact that my sorts of inherently existing phenomena necessarily function throughout the six realms of existence.

Sentient beings fabricate their reality: *they objectify each phenomenon as itself being the origin of the meaning that they have imputed.* They project their conceptualizing upon the world, and then say that those things are established truly that very way in themselves. But all of those things are their own fabrications. Just as one perceives a coil of rope as a snake or as one mistakes a far off pile of stones for a man, or takes for water what is only a mirage, one fixates upon these fabrications as truly existing just in the way that they are immediately perceived. I myself never really wanted to do all that I do, but I do them anyway, simply because it is the world that people have become accustomed to expect.

So there. I do look forward to sitting back and watching in wonder to learn what you think about all of this.

---

[1] These are matricide, patricide, killing a holy person, maliciously wounding a Buddha, and creating division among a spiritual community.

9 The Reifying Habit Scrutinizes the Practices of Scholars

The reifying habit continues by satirizing wisdom's methods of meditating:

Wisdom, you yourself never appear among what is perceived to have true existence, not in the consciousness that ascertains things nor among the objects that appear, but this does *not* prove that wisdom is non-existent. If such non-appearance was because of non-existence, then wisdom would have to be totally non-existent. That cannot be the case since in a very general way a kind of wisdom does exist. Likewise, I do not appear for the ascertainment of suchness by a meditative absorption, for which nothing has an inherent essence; but this does not prove that I am utterly non-existent. Just because I do not appear there does not mean that I do not exist at all. The non-existence of reifications is disproven by the fact that when a yogi gets up following the completion of some meditative stabilization, truly existing phenomena reappear at once everywhere, just like before. Truly existing phenomena appear not only at that time—what has been given the title, "the subtle obscurations," which are produced when one perceives phenomena to be truly existing, remain until the end of the continuum of the ten grounds on the path of a spiritual practitioner, and I myself am present as part of those cognitions. So you see, there is getting to be quite a collection of refutations to your position!

To one who is meditating upon the lack of inherent being of the physical, emotional, or mental constituents of a person, no inherent existence is ascertained, but these constituents are not non-existent. The same is true of me. The visualizations one has while perfecting the meditations of the generation path of tantra may not include an ascertainment of the gross components of a person, like the bare flesh and bones, but that does not mean that the constituents of a person do not exist at all. Likewise, I too may not appear to a meditator, but I still exist. Accordingly, your reasoning is misguided.

When people, from scholars to untrained persons, are handed a book to read, they pay more attention to who is the author of a book than they do to the book's actual subject. If they think that the author is not very good, then no matter how profoundly the topics may be treated, people will avoid the composition in the same way they avoid pigs or an emaciated dog, and they will cast the book aside along with any profound discussions it may contain. In other cases an author may be popular and have a wide reputation, so people will have confidence in what the author has written even though the reasoning may not be very profound. Even when the book does not explain matters well, people will attempt to cultivate genuine experiences based upon it, so they will mostly end up reinforcing my undertakings. As a consequence, their study will not be of much service to them. This is the destiny that faces your fine undertakings.

Clever scholars become so intensely preoccupied with the terminology within a course of argumentation that they never consider the basic topic, or the point of a book itself. While they understand a great many things, they miss the one! Not only do they fail to appreciate the principal point, they do not want others to grasp the meaning because their main purpose is to protect their own standing. This too furthers my objectives. If scholars are incapable of doing better than that, then what hope can there be that dull-witted people will grasp the meaning? What has become of all of your splendid undertakings? Their only service seems to be to augment my own practices.

Scholars may read some writers who offer informative exegeses of profound subjects and express matters succinctly, but they ignore them because the authors appear to be quite common or are attired simply. Such scholars are given to complain that the author failed to include what the scriptures said about one of the topics. Even though they may have generated some resentment toward the author, they will usually voice a few kind words; however, their own competitiveness prevents them from deeply considering the profound matters that the author may be addressing. Cannot their rejection of the profound matters be the result of the fact that the habits I have been cultivating have taken root inside their metal continuums? These efforts of theirs augment my own activities, which accumulate in opposition to your aims.

There are other scholars who previously esteemed the wholesome and profound view of their lineage teachers but then changed their opinion; they do not simply reject the lineage views, despite their profundity they disparage them because they diverge from some newly adopted views to which they become attached egotistically. Such behavior is another result of my pervasive influence, which works to effectively oppose your influence. What could be more satisfactory to me than this further expansion of my influence?

Some scholars lacking in wisdom have teachers who like to call the eastern direction west, yet these scholars consider such instruction to be profound. They accept it as true just the way they are taught. On the other hand, other teachers may grasp the profound meaning and offer wonderful explanations, but their teachings will not be studied or become the basis for any serious reflection. I am active in the mental continuums of these scholars also. If you find that many difficulties seem to be gathering about your project, know that they are all due to my activities, which are ever expanding.

When lay people and sangha alike, from a simple yak shepherd to a wise person, visit a spiritual teacher in search of some teaching, they will make an offering of food and request some profound insight about the dharma. When they don't receive what they ask for immediately, most of them will think that the teacher is incapable; that way they end up doing nothing more than cultivating methods for reducing their faith. Although they seek oral instruction about the dharma, their real purpose is to use what they may receive for increasing their wealth and reputation. This too is more of my doing, which further subdues you, for the reason that it undermines your peculiar idea that the 'I' does not truly exist.[1]

Others who display much veneration to their teachers receive all the precious and profound instruction that they have asked for, yet they become irritated about not receiving any decent butter tea, so they leave displeased. These people also end up cultivating very negative perspectives that steer them toward a miserable existence. This is more of my doing, further disproving your notion that the 'I' does not exist.

Some dharma practitioners become puffed up with pride and like to keep going around telling everyone how great the dharma is. When they finally manage to do a little practice themselves, so that there is some small indication that they have had a genuine experience (for example, a few hairs that stand-up), they are utterly convinced that they have become saintly,. and then they become eager to proselytize to anyone. Should one offer them the slightest bit of praise, their arrogance will inflate to fill up the universe, so their practice ends up only deepening their cultivation of pride. Here is even more evidence of my influence, which undermines your assertion that I do not exist.

---

[1] The Panchen Lama frequently employs an interesting polysemic trope, where the words *nga med* ("I do not exist") bear very well the *double meaning* that the 'I' does not exist *and* that the one with reifying egoistic habits does not exist. This can happen because reifying habits (*bdag 'dzin / bden 'dzin*, see Appendix II) has been personified in the dialogue of this text and frequently has been involved with some reification of the notion of 'I' along with the other notions that it habitually reifies. English does not bear this double sense of 'I' well, a situation that forces the translator to keep choosing one of these two senses and to forsake the other.

10 The Reifying Habit Assesses *Sutra* and *Tantra*

The one with reifying habits continues:

My activities are to be found everywhere, whereas yours never roam far from the dark corners where you reside. Most scholars and yogis attempt some meditation, such as visualizing themselves as one obscure form or another, and they engage their meditative objects in the way that one might watch the performance of a play, passively gazing at matters that seem to be occurring at a distance. All this is not at all incompatible with me, and merely thinking of their efforts makes me chuckle.

My activities are effective everywhere, but yours only leaves people discouraged. Preoccupied with a few words whose sense is inflated, some practitioners try to settle themselves in a decent stabilized equipoise, but when they actually meditate on selflessness they cultivate a perspective that ends up reaffirming their own existence. They usually witness the existence of themselves and their object of meditation as somehow being separate. Some of those who cultivate how entities lack inherent being think that if they do not have inherent existence they will become sheer nothingness. Instead of meditating on the nature of phenomena, they mostly engage in a variety of meditating on the present consciousness.

Others may meditate on mere clarity itself, but this is another meditation that is compatible with me. It involves preventing any thoughts from entering the mind, and naturally, this is mostly just lip service. In any event, it is not really a genuine cessation but merely a kind of suppression, one at a time, of whatever might appear. How is stopping all mental activity going to lead to undermining the way that everyone habitually reifies things?

No matter how skilled one may become at (a) describing formally what is an obsessive fixation upon entities that are perceived to have inherent being and (b) formulating what is conventionally valid, when it comes to putting all of this into practice during one's meditation, it becomes extremely difficult to differentiate between these two. Trying to discern the boundary between what contingent existence there is on the basis of customary terminology and consensual distinctions and what lacks inherent being will keep one's head spinning, and one will become fatigued without accomplishing a thing. On the other hand, my own methods are able to achieve miracles, which offer much more than any of your attempts to obtain liberation, during which a person has to go practically insane in attempting to abandon everyday life. This situation is extremely amusing to me.

There are other scholars who like to analyze formally whether a phenomenon that is purported to have inherent being can exist as an individual entity or as the composite of many entities. They analyze again and again by employing various means of highly technical reasoning, and the more strongly that they focus upon these refutations, which exhaust their minds, the more they weaken the intensity of the clarity with which they are able to maintain their focus upon a proper antidote. Weakening their clarity this way becomes another effective technique for cultivating ignorance. Having done so, when they engage in their focusing meditation they end up with a meditative absorption that keeps shifting abruptly among identifying "this exists" and "this does not exist," along with a full assortment of possibilities for explaining the lack of the self-existence of phenomena.

Some of these practitioners unwittingly fall under the sway of a bit of sluggishness, or have flurries of distracting thoughts. The worst thing about these subtle flaws is that the practitioners still think they are meditating, so the errors are able to persist for quite a long while before being recognized. When grosser varieties of mental fogginess or too many extraneous thoughts intrude and one fails to recommence from the beginning a cultivation of everything that one has missed, one will begin to *contrive* the nature of the meditative stabilization. By then one will have surrendered any hold that one may have had of a real antidote to reification, and one will be left to meditate only upon the clear and knowing characteristics of the mind. The result is that one ends up meditating upon the nature of one's own consciousness. This will place one in a very compromising position when one claims, "My 'I' has no existence."

Just as a fire that never touches firewood will not be able to get the wood to burn, practices of cultivation like this prevent one from achieving one's purpose. That kind of meditation—in which the reification of "true" appearance is never apprehended clearly and is never directly confronted by its antidote, i.e., by the realization of its being empty of any inherent nature—will not only be unable to present any hardship to me, it will only enhance my dominance. So please, you don't really need to tire yourself out in these ways! The meditative exercises I have been describing are scholars' battlegrounds, and people who are untrained will end up dumbfounded with their heads spinning. Are you now able to see how effective all of my activities are? Wisdom, these intricate battlegrounds are where you get completely stuck.

What kind of appearances do these contemplative stabilizations actually ascertain? They discover only the appearances of more things that have inherent existence. Even when they witness the emptiness of reality, *they reify that very lack of inherent existence itself* as if it was yet one more "truly" existing phenomenon, so there is never any scope for them to improve their outlook upon their experience. If there are any flaws in the way that one determines the lack of the inherent existence of empty reality, then what one ascertains will either still exist inherently or it will be utterly non-existent.

If one claims that one is ascertaining nothing, then what sort of meditative stabilization can come about? If one replies that it is a focused meditation on the emptiness that negates inherent existence, then notions either appear in the focusing meditation or they do not appear. If they appear, then the faults that I've just finished outlining will reoccur, i.e., one will turn them into one more thing that exists with an inherent essence. If they do not appear, then it means that any thoughts that have gathered in the mind are erased the moment that they reach there. From my perspective, it is impossible to differentiate between a meditation upon a mind that has been pacified and a meditation upon nothing whatsoever. How are you possibly able to distinguish these meditations from each other?

If you reply that the lack of inherent existence that you ascertain is different than either of these, and that discussing whether consciousness exists in a general way or not makes no contribution to our consideration of *inherent* existence, then I need to ask you whether consciousness exists during your cultivation of meditative stabilization. If you claim that the consciousness that is ascertaining reality exists, then it follows that there is some inherent existence there; hence, I too must exist. If you claim that nothing at all exists, then you are cultivating nothing that is capable of possessing an antidote for correcting obsessive reifications. For this reason you will continue to be unable to harm me.

If you say that you are exceptionally vigilant in maintaining a firm hold of the ascertainment that I lack any inherent essence, then just exactly *who* is this person who is being so vigilant? It is entirely possible that that mind may be the one that does not exist! Just where does this mind that is so vigilant exist? As soon as the meditative stabilization has any objective content, reification has necessarily been at work! Or, if reification is truly absent, how can one engage in cultivating anything at all? If you claim that while nothing is ascertained during the meditation and that the consciousness of the lack of inherent being occurs just prior to the meditative stabilization, then that realization would not be able to contribute anything to being vigilant during the meditative stabilization itself. If you claim that it occurs following the completion of some meditative stabilization, then how can it be relevant during the meditation? And if you say that it occurs during the meditative stabilization itself, then that may be so, but precisely what are the boundaries of where it enters and exits, and upon what is it founded? If you say that meditative stabilization itself is its own basis, then it must be that meditative stabilization is equivalent to emptiness; but that would mean that emptiness is *both* the support and the supported. It cannot be that the mind itself has become emptiness because if the mind is equivalent to emptiness, then the most that it can be is a chimera. But if that is not the case, the mind that is established in meditative stabilization will surely be unable to avoid cultivating me.

If you contend that there is some kind of derivative mind that is able to produce a meditative stabilization upon the main mind while the main mind is meditating upon the emptiness, then where does this derivative mind reside? If you say that it has a place during the meditative stabilization, the previous faults apply in the way I have just explained. If you claim that the derivative mind exists during the meditation "in an unmanifested way," that is very much like what those non-Buddhists who accept the existence of principal causes, like a soul, try to argue.

Perhaps you would like to compete with the Sāmkhya whose position we are always challenging and for which we offer the absurd consequence that a sprout must always already be present inside the seed "in an unmanifested way" before it germinates, an illustration that represents how the Sāmkhya invent an entity has an inherent being that endures and is self-produced. If you choose to argue in this way, the Sāmkhya may begin to grow jealous of you.

Some of those who meditate like this are extremely confused. Even if one spends one's entire lifetime assiduously cutting off every single thought that arises in one's mind, what will actually never arise is an effective result. My habits of reifying one's practices are already inscribed in even these activities. It offers further proof of my influence, again contradicting your assertion that I do not exist.

If one does not know just when to apply reasoning and just when to abide in a stabilized realization of what one has analyzed, then all of these investigations will only cause your head to spin. Too much analysis can become excessive and become one more defective practice; however, not applying reason at all is an even greater flaw. One needs to become very skilled at knowing when to apply formal analysis and when to cease applying it, and one must develop an exceptional aptitude for using reason in apposite ways.

Have you considered that while you have been cutting off each and every thought, just once you might have had a small realization that is worth retaining? If you keep cutting off every idea, when you are cultivating a profound mantra like OM SVABHĀVA SHUDDHA SARVA DHARMA SVABHĀVA SHUDDO HUM, which expresses, "All phenomena have a self-nature that is pure, and my nature is pure!" how are you going to be able to develop the divine pride[1] that you have generated by thinking "My nature is pure"?

Does that divine pride exist during this meditative stabilization upon the pure nature of all phenomena, or not? If you say that it does, then that pride would have to be a mundane identification. Then it would be a pride about me! But if you really feel this sort of inherent pride, how will you be able to cultivate a nature that is truly pure? And if you don't feel this pride, how will you be able to develop a proper focusing meditation upon it? If the pride, which is an aspect of customary reality, is part of the focus during a meditative stabilization upon the pure nature and you are saying that it is the basic aspect of pure nature to be empty, then the mundane identification part and the emptiness part must be residing together somehow. But how can that be possible?

If divine pride has become empty, then no one will be able to hold on to it. If the emptiness has become divine pride, then it is no longer a real emptiness. Therefore, there must either be no emptiness or no pride. If there is no emptiness, there can be no meditation upon emptiness. If there is no pride, then there will be no divine pride to engage in cultivating emptiness. If you say that the two are mixed together, it would become like some illusory object, and only a very peculiar meditative practice would be cultivating the emptiness of that sort of thing. If divine pride were to appear to anyone with that kind of meditation, it is for sure it would be my own practice of customary reification that is appearing. And since I always keep people's company anyway, being the very reliable friend that I am, there is not really any need to deliberately cultivate me.

Since we are speaking about "all phenomena," should not my pride, i.e. myself, be included there, with all the rest? If you claim confidently that it is, then must not this pride of mine also share the aspect of the pure nature of emptiness? If so, how is there a problem of fixating upon any mundane sort of pride? If you do assert that there was any mundane aspect to pride that was existing in its continuum, even that continuity of pride must still be something that is included in the category of "all phenomena" that your mantra boasts about. How can you suggest that there is anything that can be excluded from being part of "everything"? On the other hand, if the pride that you claim you are perceiving has not become united with emptiness and instead you are gazing at emptiness like someone who gazes out at a performance, then there is no proper cultivation of the lack of inherent being, and what you perceive will be ineffective at undermining me.

Wisdom, my arguments seem to have taken your breath away! Are you growing so weary of all this that you are finding it difficult to say anything?

When one is absorbed in the invocation of the "ŚŪNYATĀ" mantra,[2] it embodies how the subject and the empty object share one indivisible nature. When one proclaims, "I AM THAT NATURE," just who is the subject that is being cultivated there, and what sort of pride can it have? If the mind of an active subject and the pride being construed involve nothing more than a conventionally designated 'I,' is the meditative stabilization on emptiness positing pride there, or not? If pride is there, then I'm there too! But if there is no pride there, then who is it who is capable of being proud? If the pride and the emptiness are inextricably mixed, does that mean that at the time you are witnessing emptiness there is pride then too? If so, then the object of that meditation necessarily involves an aspect of reification. Accordingly, if an indivisible emptiness permeates everything, then the pride too must have become empty. If that is so, two contradictory phenomena will be forced to abide together; however, such a theory must be mistaken, as I have already argued.

If you claim that neither pride nor emptiness are absent and that they abide together as an appearance and its emptiness, that would be an explanation that can apply to a practical system for preserving such a realization during the period following a meditative stabilization, not to what must occur during the actual meditative experience itself. How could it possibly be describing an actual meditative absorption that realizes mere emptiness! Your head must once again be beginning to spin trying to figure out the boundaries between meditation and post-meditation, and between analytic meditation and placement meditation, which is additional evidence that the influence of my activities is very extensive. Could it be that you, wisdom, are beginning to grow jealous of me?

Some practitioners who must contend with all of this are not capable of figuring it all out. They may blame their confusion upon the tantric practices and think it might require some sort of peculiar tantra that is free of any content. When NĀDA[3] has dissolved into clear light and a vast empty clarity has become the meditative focus, just what can that empty clarity be?[4] In increasingly subtle stages, each supporting element is absorbed into what it had been supporting,[5] until nothing is left but the NĀDA, which attracts all of the mental focus. The result of the absorption of the visualization of the mandala and the gradual dissolution of the deity and the seed syllable at deity's heart is a vast empty clarity, which is the fundamental basis upon which the mind relies. How are you ever going to be able to distinguish the fine line that separates the result of this process of gradual dissolution into empty clarity and the emptiness that results from removing every single thought that may arise in the mind?

Although you claim to be able to make such fine distinctions, you are not able to differentiate the practice of cutting off everything that appears to the mind from the practice of integrating the appearances into the vast empty clarity. The latter method is the only way to cultivate the lack of inherent essences and is the proper antidote that undermines my objectifying habits; but since you cannot tell one from the other, you are unable to challenge me effectively.

During this practice once the full mandala is visualized as having no inherent being, by subtle stages the mandala dissolves into suchness, in the form of that vast empty clarity in which there is no apprehension of any inherent being. Although you claim that this will constitute an antidote that is capable of undermining me, the notion that a cultivation of some total nothingness is going to establish the lack of inherent being of a person that has been customarily and continuously identified in a concretized way for infinite millennia is nothing more than empty talk. Having cultivated a successful visualization on one occasion, such a person may again act out a simulation of an effective practice, thinking, "My habitual mode of perceiving, which is the antidote that opposes you, witnesses no inherent essences." But if during the meditative stabilization there is no proper cultivation of an active opposing mode of apprehending things, then despite all of your proud declarations about the wonderful meditations you are having, nothing will be accomplished. Those practices will not be capable of doing a person any more good than would all of the roasted barley flour one has kept stored at home at the time one finds oneself on the road hungry and without any food.

Some practitioners conceive the NĀDA and mind to be separate from each other. During the process of dissolution, one's mind gazes out at events as if one was nothing more than a spectator who sits and observes whatever happens, while the NĀDA merges into some vast empty clarity. Just what is that kind of meditation good for?

Other practitioners may argue that the mind and the NĀDA are entirely inseparable, especially while the NĀDA is being visualized to be merging into the vast empty clarity. But even in that situation the mind must still have to sit back as a spectator, if only for the reason that after the NĀDA itself dissolves, the mind will still be left behind. If, however, you wish to argue that the mind is totally inseparable from the NĀDA's pure nature, which is without any inherent being, and so the mind must dissolve along with the NĀDA, then I suppose that you would argue also that when a person is cremated and the body is badly singed, the mind would also be singed? And when the body is fully consumed, would you likewise contend that the mind would be fully consumed? Hence, when the NĀDA finally perishes one would be unable to generate a mind that could perceive that vast empty clarity. That position seems very similar to the view of one of the lower schools of Buddhism.[6]

Do you disagree with this? During your practice of visualizing the disappearing of the NĀDA, which is construed as the lack of any inherent being, how are you formulating the meaning of the lack of inherent being? Is the disappearing of a pile of clouds that rolls across a clear blue sky equivalent to the empty mode of the cloud's actual being? Is the disappearance of the NĀDA as it is visualized equivalent to the emptiness of the mind? The situation of the actual being of the mind is similar to the cloud in that it consists of having no inherent essence from its own side, but you need to identify precisely the actual nature of the mind's emptiness and do more than simply base it upon a general sort of emptiness. Claiming that emptiness is nothing at all would only make it easier for me to function.

All phenomena may be analyzed this way–they exist, but they are empty of having inherent essences.[7] When people do not have a firm understanding of what emptiness actually is, when they operate without the guidance of a teacher and practice in any way they please, they will remain wandering about endlessly in their repetitive and superficial everyday lives. Therefore, you must rely upon a learned teacher. However, by itself even such reliance is insufficient. One must develop *for oneself* an always active self-understanding that reflexively ascertains and examines each reifying projection in its particular details. Although one abides in that awareness, one should not become satisfied with that formal understanding of emptiness but continue to actively exercise one's analytic faculties to expose and remove all of the innate tendencies to reify phenomena. This is the way to employ the benefits of leisure and prosperity meaningfully. I, the habit of reification, am giving you some straight talk here. You are too full of yourself, wisdom; however, your bragging is able to fill up the universe for no longer than a brief instant.

If all you sentient beings in the three realms follow wisdom yet keep circling endlessly from one mundane existence to another, will you not by yourselves conceive that I am real? How can you persist in denying that I have any inherent existence? It seems to me that you should at least have the courage of your own convictions and stop your fixating upon what has no inherent existence as if the lack of inherent existence is the only thing that does have an inherent essence.

---

[1] This is a unique pride that one cultivates during a practice of tantric meditation and that involves abandoning one's egoistic self-image and replacing it with the self-image of the deity or *yidam* who is the basis of one's meditative practice.

[2] "Śūnyatā" is Sanskrit for emptiness. The mantra is "OM ŚŪNYATĀ JNANA VAJRA SVABHĀVA ATMAKO HUM" ("Om Emptiness, the indestructible wisdom; I am that nature!")

[3] The "NĀDA" is the last remaining graphic element of a seed syllable inside the heart of the *yidam* (the meditative deity), which is used at an advanced stage of a meditation as the focal point of the meditative concentration. Barely a squiggle, it is the most subtle part of the visualization, and it is imagined as being absorbed into emptiness. During this portion of the tantric practice, a yogi experiences an overwhelming sense of emptiness, which is described as a vast empty clarity (*stong sang*), which several lamas have rendered in their colloquial English as "clean-clear."

[4] This question includes consideration of the matter of whether the empty clarity is an emptiness of appearances or an emptiness of inherent existence.

[5] The mandala with the celestial mansion is absorbed into the meditative deities who are joined in union; the consort is dissolved into the principal meditative deity, who is further absorbed into the seed syllable that sits on a sun-seat at the deity's heart; finally, one element at a time each supporting component of the seed syllable dissolves into the graphic element that it supports until all that remains is the vertical "squiggle" of the NĀDA, which sits above the

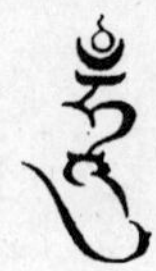

seed syllable. The NĀDA itself then dissolves into emptiness:.

[6] The reference here is to the *bye brag smra ba* (Tib.) or *Vaibhāśika* (Skt.), who believe that when the constituents of a person cease (i.e., the five aggregated physical, emotional, and mental components of a sentient being), the consciousness that perceives those constituents must also cease. As Khensur Lobsang Tsering explained, for the *bye brag smra ba* school any consciousness must have a body. Further, there seems to be a dialectical relation at work between the object and the subject here—the cessation of the object, i.e., the NĀDA, would entail the cessation of the subject, the perceiving mind. The notion that the mind could be consumed along with the body [a simpler rendering of "constituent" (*pung po*)] is much more controversial for Tibetans than it is for most readers of English, since it would mean that the mind would be unable to take subsequent rebirth.

[7] The illustration alluded to in the previous paragraph, of a pile of clouds hanging in a valley, is especially apt. As a cloud stretches across an empty sky, the water molecules spread apart, until they disappear from view. They still exist, but there is no longer any "cloud." That cloud does not have an inherent being. As the water molecules keep rolling across the valley to the mountain range on the other side, the water molecules once again condense, and a cloud reappears. The cloud has existence by virtue of its interconnected dependence upon the causes (the water molecules, which have their own interconnectedly dependent being) and the conditions (the sky, the mountain, and the breeze carrying the cloud), but the cloud bears no *inherent* existence in itself. In this example, the cloud's disappearance itself is not a total emptiness of the cloud—the cloud has more existence than that. In the same way, it can be suggested that the mind has more existence than the visualized dissolution of the NĀDA into vast empty clarity.

11 Wisdom Answers with an Illustration

Wisdom replies:

You certainly have a great deal to say about divine pride, and you have raised a quite a number of topics regarding it, but I'm going to offer you a very simple reply that will address all of those aspects at once. So sit and listen carefully, and then give me your honest response. I will offer an illustration that is capable of resolving these matters and that will assist you in giving a fully informed reply.

Take two cups that are half-filled with water. When one mixes one cup into the other will it still be possible to distinguish one cup's water from the other? If you say that it is, then by all means please go ahead and try. If you say you cannot, then has the water in the first half-cup become lost somewhere in the water of the second half-cup? If it has, then just what has become of "the water in the first half-cup" and "the water of the second half-cup"? Is it possible to continue to use these names for distinguishing them? If you say that it is, then which is the part that is "the water in the first half-cup"? If you say that it is not, are you willing to deny that it was the water of the first half-cup that filled the second cup? At the time that that water was poured, there was a difference regarding the waters that were combined in the cup, and that difference can be named. Since there is a difference that can be named, it would contradict any assertion that no distinction can be made. The very same applies to one's meditation.

If you claim that only subsequent to the cups of water being mixed is it that there no longer a basis for distinguishing them, then at the time of the actual mixing itself, would you assert that the water of the first half-cup exists or not? If it does not exist at that time, then how is it that the pouring caused the second cup to become so very full? If the first half-cup does exist at the time of the mixing, but you maintain that later it does not, then it follows that this non-existence that cannot be discerned must be existing in some unmanifested way. If that has become your position, then the logic of your argument is undermined, and you are the one who is making the same kind of argument that the Sāmkhya do, which is what you have just accused me of doing.

The divine pride of a *chos sku* operates in an analogous way. Like both half-cups of water that are combined, neither the subject that experiences great bliss nor its object, emptiness, has an identity that can be differentiated, but they exist. When one proclaims during one's mantra recitation, "I AM THAT" and generates divine pride, which is an aspect of the *chos sku*, one establishes oneself in the nature of emptiness in a way that is similar to how the water of one cup was poured into the second cup. The divine pride that has merged with emptiness does not appear to one who is established in meditative stabilization; nevertheless, during the process of the meditative stabilization it exists there. How could one possibly identify it? The subject who is experiencing great bliss also exists, just as the water does in the illustration.

So when does one apprehend the divine pride? One apprehends it during the meditative stabilization, and the method is that the apprehending is itself *its own basis*. The subject experiencing great bliss and the object, emptiness, are indistinguishable; they have one taste. One's nature is that very "I AM," and the mode of apprehending the divine pride is a thoroughgoing negation of inherent being that does not implicitly affirm anything. It has the characteristic of an intense lucidity. With extraordinary aptitude one should apply incisive concentration and maintain the continuity of this meditative stabilization, while guarding against any excitement or lethargy.

During this practice sometimes yogis are able to employ in effective ways the energy of their sexuality. There is no way to express this unique experience. Like a mute person who has dreamed a dream, one cannot describe this experience. You cannot understand such things. You may hear about them, but since you are ignorant about them you probably will not believe them anyway. Besides, these matters are secret, and I should not really be speaking about them in any detail in front of you.

The initial dissolution of the celestial mansion, the deity, the seed syllable, and the NĀDA, and also the subsequent absorption into emptiness are not meditations upon utter nothingness; rather, they result in the dawning of clear light, a view of suchness that permits every phenomenon to be revealed lucidly in the way that the light of the sun is able to dispel darkness. The light of this wisdom removes the obscuration produced by having fixed the truths of constructed entities. This mode of cognition is a negation only, and it does not implicitly affirm anything about what is being negated. One's task is to maintain firmly the continuity of a meditative stabilization that has activated this incisively focused lucidity, which is given the designation "clear light." The mind and the NĀDA are indistinguishable from each other and become the clear light that has fused with emptiness.

The light of this wisdom dispels the darkness that results from the mind's having fixated upon its truth habits and reveals the mind's actual mode of being. Having explained these matters to you, with all of your habits of fixating truths, perhaps I am able to shut you up at last. Since you are confused about just what is the mode of being of phenomena, "ignorance" is a particularly apt appellation for you. I shine like the sun and the moon in the sky, whose mere appearance eliminates darkness, whereas you are left always puzzling like some bewildered sheep, are you not? So what need would *you* ever have for the NĀDA?

Let me explain to you just how the meditation concerning the NĀDA functions. The celestial mansion of the mandala with its foundations and levels that support the NĀDA provide a mode of reflection that serves as an antidote that undermines the habitual, typical ways that we fixate upon phenomena. It does that by developing an ascertaining consciousness that understands well that there is no inherent being to the body or to the mind; and we are able to appreciate the emptiness of the ways we have fixated upon phenomena, i.e., our truth habits, thereby revealing just the way things are. The various aspects of the bases of the mandala and what each base supports are no longer apprehended as mundane forms with inherent essences; instead, as the mandala dissolves, everything that appears becomes a source for apprehending the emptiness of inherent nature. By meditating upon the gods' and goddesses' bodies we are able to bring to an end to the absolutism of mundane appearances. There is only an ascertainment of the gods' and goddesses' embodiments of emptiness, and no longer are there any mundane bodies with apparently true existence.

While nothing having inherent existence is ascertained, it is not that the mundane forms have no existence at all. If nothing whatsoever appeared, it would become some nihilistic denial of existence. Although the appearance that something really exists is not extinguished, the cultivation of the ascertained body of a deity permits one to develop a stable, nondual environment that progressively extends its presence, completely reversing the way that things appear when they are believed to exist by virtue of their own inherent essences. Like a pair of scales, the more that one stabilizes a realization of the lack of inherent being, the more the appearance of inherent essences is diminished. Further, each reified object is revealed just the way it is as soon as the perspective of emptiness causes the dualistic appearances side of the scales to crash to the bottom.

The antidote that can deconstruct your habitual mode of reifying entities is available. Unfortunately, you have no way of understanding anything about it, so you keep trying to peddle the idea that you are a great benefactor, like you were some kind of big deal. The indivisible mind-cum-NĀDA that appears has no inherent being, and once it merges with the clear light awareness, there is no longer any scope for your obsessive habit of reifying each notion you entertain!

This emptiness that has merged with the clear light is the antidote known as suchness, and it blazes brightly like a great fire. So long as that fire is blazing, you can keep feeding it the fuel of whatever deluded notions you have, and it will only grow stronger. Once you understand the details of this unique method, you should use it as a rich resource that you can apply in every situation.

12 Debating the Extremes of Positivism and Nihilism

The reifying habit considers the gap between wisdom's words and the actual meditative practices of cultivating wisdom:

What a fine rosary of words you are able to spin when you debate! But they are not informed by an accurate understanding. You know just how to use the right terminology with skill, and you pontificate perfectly about how meditation should be performed. You even seem eager to do a bit of meditative practice yourself, and it is difficult to criticize you or to find fallacies in your wording. However, when it comes time to actually meditate, you and some of these great yogis have no idea how to go about organizing your practice. You recite this thing and that, but it amounts to nothing much, and you are always uncertain about just what it is you're supposed to be doing next. Moreover, your meditative practice is unable to successfully distinguish between the lack of inherent being and utter non-existence. If you are incapable of discerning *this* difference during your meditation, what simply exists and what exists with an inherent essence will remain indistinguishable. The result will be that you will continue to dwell in the two extremes of positivism and nihilism. I myself would very much like to learn more about those kind of methods!

If during your meditation you are incapable of distinguishing what exists with an inherent essence and what simply exists, your refined terminology will be of little benefit to you. If you cannot distinguish these matters during your actual meditative practice when it counts, then your head is destined to keep spinning about inside of its bafflement. If you claim that during your practice you are indeed able to make these critical distinctions, then kindly present those details to me.

Regarding this matter of my not having any inherent existence, it is only what you are able to establish during your meditative stabilization that can be effective. When you are settled on a cultivation of an emptiness of inherent existence that uses me as its basis, although no inherent essence can be there do I exist there or not? If do appear there, then since I have some nature that exists, some positivism would be implicated, is that not so? But if I do not exist there at all, what sense can there be to meditating upon my lack of existence? It seems you are condemned either to positivism or nihilism.

If you claim that in the face of your established meditative stabilization there is no inherent existence but something exists only during the process of meditation itself, then at least at that time I would have to exist there. In that case, it would still be a meditative stabilization upon me. How is it that you can use my inescapable existence there to establish a meditation on my non-existence? If you say that I do not exist even during the process of meditation, then you will surely have fallen into a nihilistic view, will you not? In that circumstance who will be capable of cultivating any proper lack of inherent existence? Please explain to me what kind of emptiness it is that has no basis that is empty.

If the 'I' has been purified by being absorbed into the emptiness during the "I AM THAT NATURE" portion of the practice, since the 'I' exists as one part of that 'I'-and-emptiness-nature that are indistinguishable, the 'I' must still exist too; however, no one will be able to determine just what sort of existence it has or be able to differentiate between its inherent and non-inherent being. If your meditation cannot locate where or how the 'I' exists, then how will there be any productive cultivation of its lack of inherent existence? Practice like that is very compatible with my kind of stabilization.

You are clueless, wisdom, and it is possible that in this way you will unknowingly be devoting your extensive meditative training to cultivating inherent existence, yet you still have high hopes of achieving the *chos sku.* That would be a very strange sequence of cause and result. With thinking like that, you are yourself more ignorant than I am! Thinking that any confused cultivation, which can just as easily become a cultivation of inherent existence, can be conducive to bringing about the *chos sku* is ridiculous. Otherwise, since everyone has been cultivating inherent existence throughout time, why have they not been able to attain liberation already, without having to make any additional effort. Meditations like these are my allies, and these days most practitioners seem to be engaging in such kinds of practice.

People like to mouth a few words about how earnestly they are cultivating my lack of existence, but just like a termite who lives in the center of a log, turning the log into nothing while it eats it out from the inside, I remain established there at the very center of the practitioner's object of meditation. Consequently, the more that they cultivate practices that tacitly employ the assumption that entities have inherent existence, the more that I myself–the habit of reifying every notion–will flourish. Your methods have failed to determine any precise way to avoid positivism and nihilism, so your methods will only use up your energy, without producing any result.

Wisdom gives his final reply:

I have carefully explained the profound meaning of these matters to you; however, no matter how well I keep clarifying things, you find it difficult to comprehend the meaning. You examine matters carefully only for the purpose of identifying mistakes and errors. Moreover, you are like those people who are inclined to deceive others and so talk a great deal; you offer much chatter even though your understanding is quite minimal. Despite being clueless, and perhaps because of it, you are full of self-admiration. You are the kind that pays special attention to how an author composes the wording, preserves the rhythmic structure, correctly keeps the lines metrical, and so forth, but you find it difficult to comprehend the meaning of what is written. Even so, you have at least given me some basis for clearing up a few doubts.

Although you yourself do not really think your understanding of these matters is very deep, you are very quick to give a smart answer. Your only course is to abandon this preoccupation with identifying all of the mistakes in others' thinking, listen carefully to what I am about to tell you now, and then closely examine all of these matters anew.

Just as one adds kindling to a fire to make it blaze, so do appearances increase the fire of one's meditative stabilization; and just as the fire consumes the firewood, the meditative stabilization surely consumes those illusory appearances. While the fire of the meditative stabilization is active, this firewood keeps increasing its flame.[1] The firewood exists, for without such firewood how would the fire remain vigorous? As the blaze grows stronger, the meditation becomes more stable, and by its conclusion all of the firewood is consumed by its flames. In that way the notions of inherent existence that have been reified by the reificatory practices serve to increase the light of the roaring fire of wisdom, which blazes throughout the meditative stabilization until it witnesses no further appearance of reifications. How can that be considered utterly non-existing?

The lack of being that is evident to meditative stabilization is a lack of *inherent* essences in phenomena, so how can you possibly claim that it will lead to nihilism? Nihilist extremism entails a denial of any situationally contingent consensus regarding terminological conventions for understanding the local efficacy of phenomena.[2] Although reifications are not witnessed by the meditative stabilization, they do exist during the process of meditation itself, where they feed the light-giving fire of wisdom.[3] If they did not exist during that time, no matter how large the fire was how would the firewood of the reified notions of inherent existence ever get to be burned? Other than consuming that particular fuel, there is no other way for wisdom to keep its fire burning.

For you to accuse this of being nihilism is as confused as one who participates in the ritual offering of a body to the west for a flesh-eating demon who lives in the east, or like inspecting the woods thoroughly for the tracks of a thief who has already fled to the plains: you are baffled by basic causal relations, and you seem surprised by the simple statement, "It burns up." Even you should be able to understand this illustration and its meaning, if you put some persistent effort into it.

For one who is established in meditative stabilization, the 'I' has no inherent essence. Although the 'I' does not appear, the nihilistic extreme is dispelled without having to accept any positivism. Because the 'I' that is empty of any inherent essence has a basis that does exist, there is not a complete denial of being. You need to pay better attention: the 'I' exists during the process of meditating upon how that mode of existence has no inherent being. It has to exist there; there is no other way to perform this meditative practice. But any extreme positivist view is avoided.

This is the way to cultivate the lack of inherent being. Your illustration about you being like a termite that lives in the center of the log, turning the wood into nothing whatsoever, is unsuitable here. That would apply only to a meditation that fails to properly cultivate a lack of inherent being. If during the meditative stabilization itself the 'I' has no being at all, who could possibly cultivate the *lack* of inherent being? Are you proposing that there can be an emptiness without having anything that is empty? Therefore, I have defeated you![4] It has been established clearly that your argument is illogical; nevertheless, you feel no humiliation.

The contradictions internal to your position have been revealed, but you have no inhibition about making more of these same arguments. You fit the root meanings of both "self-delusion" and "ignorance" to perfection. Whereas I am speaking the truth, you offer tricks and falsehoods, which is the reason why your and others' heads continue to spin about in confusion. Please renounce your falsehoods and speak the truth! Those lies cannot survive the truth, which is like the sunrise that gloriously illuminates the landscape.

---

[1] In this passage there is some extraordinary word play in the Panchen Lama's text, involving the Tibetan word for firewood or kindling (*bud shing*; *shing* = wood), and the elegance of this word play cannot be conveyed in the English. In three stanzas of text, the word *shing* occurs seven times, with the homonym "*zhing*" used once (meaning "and") and another time used as a gerundial participle ("-ing"), making for a total of nine instances of the homonym. Interspersed with these is the use of "blaze" (*'bar*) six times. The result is extremely elegant Tibetan, making it perfectly suitable for what is part of a concluding argument of the text. What makes this masterful style difficult to render in English is that elegance in Tibetan is frequently accomplished by repeating the same sound, and the more the number of repetitions the more elegant it becomes, whereas in English taste requires that lexical selection *avoid* repetition. Consequently, it is practically impossible to render the attractions of the Tibetan text into English, and so the elegance is not evident to the reader of the text here. Nevertheless, the metaphor by itself, which can be presented, is an effective one.

[2] *Tha snyad.*

[3] Note that the Panchen Lama maintains that there is an important difference between the process of meditation (*myam gzhag dus*) and what the resulting meditative stabilization witnesses (*mnyam gzhag mthar. ngor*).

[4] See the discussion of *skhor gsum* in the Introduction, footnote 4.

Concluding Remarks

Although the intellect of the author resembles the scope of a small frog,[1] I have composed this text in order to delight those who have a spirit of inquiry, in the way that a trailside cairn that marks a mountain pass can lift people's spirits, and also for the purpose of increasing the author's own understanding of these matters.[2] If I have upset any great scholars, then please forgive me; and may you offer me your patience, founded upon your realization of emptiness. Kindly assist me to overcome any shortcomings.

This text was written by the monk Lobsang Chökyi Gyaltsen, whose words were written for the purpose of fostering virtue and well being.

The Victorious One has highly praised
those who have had the excellent fortune to train
 in solitary retreat,
where they learn how to ground their three doors[3]
upon the pure foundation of a tamed mind,
and who, despite the unbearable degeneration that
 plagues our time,
apply their body, speech and mind exclusively to
 virtuous activities.

The actual enemy is the persistent habit of reifying each notion that one has, which has relegated all of the suffering sentient beings to becoming trapped in the ocean of their superficial and repetitive existence from time immemorial to the present. This enemy can be completely pulverized by this Debate between Wisdom and the Reifying Habit, *The Blazing Wheel of Thunderbolts That Split Asunder the Rocky Mountain of Egoistic Habits*, the printing of which was made possible by some faithful benefactors who generously sponsored the carving of its wooden print blocks. May the virtue accumulated thereby cause the holders of the dharma to live long lives.

May the harmony and pure discipline of the virtuous sects and communities increase both their theoretical understanding and their effective practice in a manner indistinguishable from that of the waxing moon. May all sentient beings, including these kind sponsors, rely upon genuine spiritual guides and come to master the Buddhist doctrine as comprehensively as a conquering army overtakes a territory; and may they soon occupy the capital city known as buddhahood.

SARVA MAŃGALAM[4]

---

[1] The Panchen Lama's reference here is to a familiar tale in Buddhist folk tradition: a frog living in the bottom of a well has grown very proud of how extensive is the pool of water where he dwells. Even though he has never visited any place outside of the well, he imagines that his pool is a great body of water, and when others try to convince him that it is really quite small, he remains skeptical, until some friends finally take him to visit the ocean.

[2] The interpretation of this passage relies upon the commentary by Lobsang Jinpa (nd: 86), from which a few words were borrowed in order to make these extremely dense lines intelligible.

[3] The three doors are the body, speech, and mind.
[4] "May all discover well being" (Sanskrit).

Appendix One: Outline of Text

(Based upon the commentary to *bdag 'dzin gshags 'debs* by Lobsang Jinpa)

1. Introduction (3/ 260)[1]
  1.1 Praises (3/ 260)
  1.2 The Point (4/ 260)
2. The Exegesis (4/ 260)
  2.1 The Basis, Path, and Result of the Great Mudra (4/ 260)
    2.11 The Basis (4/ 260)
      2.111 From the perspective of sutra (4/260.2-260.4)
      2.112 From the perspective of tantra (5/261.3-4)
    2.12 The Path (6/ 261)
      2.121 From the perspective of sutra (6/ 260.4-262.1)
      2.122 From the perspective of tantra (6/ 261.3-262.1)
    2.13 The Result (7/ 262.1-5)
  2.2 The Debate between Wisdom and the Reifying Habit (8/ 262)
    2.21 Transitional comment (8/ 262.6-262.3)
    2.22 The actual debate (9/ 263)
      2.221 Brief summary (9/ 263.3-264.1)
        2.2211 The way the one with reifying habits loves and nurtures those who practice it (9/ 263.3-264.1)
        2.2212 Wisdom's making a rebuttal (9/ 264.1-264.3)
      2.222 Extended Explanation (10/ 264)
        2.2221 *Debating the existence or non-existence, in either conventionally conceived or ultimate ways, of the*

objects conceived by the one with reifying habits (10)

2.22211 The mode of existence of the conventionally conceived object as reified by the reifying habit (10/264.3-265.2)

2.22212 Wisdom's stating the manner of non-existence of objects either as conventionally conceived or as ultimate (11/ 265.2-266.6)

2.2222 *Debating the duration of its friendship with the mind* (13/ 266)

2.22221 The position of the one with reifying habits (13/ 266)

2.222211 The way that the mind and the reifying habit have been friends continuously (13/ 266.6-268.5)

2.222212 How the mind and wisdom only have a sporadic friendship (14/ 268.5-289.2)

2.22222 Wisdom's refutation (15/ 269)

2.222221 When one investigates the reasoning that examines just the way things are, the object reified by truth habits is not apprehended (15/ 269.2-272.5)

2.222222 When one does not inspect or analyze carefully, common sense has merely a terminological basis (15/ 272.4-275.5)

2.2223 *Debating the ability and strength of the reifying habit* (21/ 275.5)

2.22231 An extensive articulation of the position of the one with reifying habits (21/ 275)

2.222311 The way that many great meditators fail to understand the system of cultivating selflessness and so are incapable of undermining it (21/ 275.5-288.1)

2.222312 Anyone who refutes that the physical, emotional, and mental aspects of personal being have inherent essences will the reifying habit; however, it occurs as frequently as a star that shines during the daytime (22/ 288.2-298.2)

2.222313 The reasons why those who practice in accordance with the ways that the schools below the Formal Analytic Reasoning Middle Way School (*Svatantrika*; *Dbu ma rang rgyud pa*) explain their philosophical views will be unable to harm the reifying habit, which will render them powerless to even liberate beings (22/ 298.2-301.4)

2.22232 Wisdom's brief reply (22/ 301.1-302.1)

2.2224 *Debating the extent of the followers and the activities of the reifying habit* (34/ 302)

2.22241 The position of the one with reifying habits (34/ 302.1)

2.222411 The way that all sentient beings are compliant with the reifying habit's directions (34/ 302.1-306.2)

2.222412 The way the 84,000 afflictive emotions are his friends (34/ 306.2-5)

2.22242 Wisdom's refutation (35)

2.222421 The unsuitable way to present actions and agents that transcend the repetitive and superficial existence of everyday life from the perspective of those who accept that phenomena have inherent existence (35/ 306.5-315.2)

2.222422 The suitable way to present actions and agents that transcend the repetitive and superficial existence of everyday life from the perspective of those who accept that phenomena are empty of inherent existence (35/ 315.2-330.2)

2.2225 *Debating how many friends and associates they each have* (44)

2.22251 The reifying habit presents his position (44/ 330.2-334.1)

2.22252 Wisdom gives his rebuttal (44)

2.222521 All phenomena that arise from the interconnected relations of causes and conditions are wisdom's friend (44/ 334.1-336.5)

2.222522 How appearance and emptiness reinforce each other (44/ 336.5-334.5)

2.2226 *Debating whether or not both exist in the continuums of ordinary beings* (50)

2.22261 The reifying habit presents his position (50)

2.222611 The one with reifying habits presents the rationale that explains why he exists in the mental continuum of beings and wisdom does not (50/ 344.5-351.1)

2.222612 Debating the system by which one can maintain the view of both sutra and tantra (50/ 351.1-371.3)

2.22262 Wisdom gives his rebuttal (50/ 371.3-377.3)

2.223 Summary (75)

2.2231 *The reifying habit presents its position* (75)

2.22311 If anything exists in the face of meditative stabilization upon emptiness, it would be a positivist extreme (75/ 377.3-378.6)

2.22312 If nothing exists at all, it would be a nihilist extreme (77/ 378.6-379.6)

2.22313 Explanation, with an illustration, for the system of cultivating the view of great yogis who do not receive instructions (79/ 379.6-380.2)

2.2232 *Wisdom gives his rebuttal* (79)

2.22321 An explanation, with illustration, of why it is not nihilism if no 'I' exists in the view of a comprehensive meditative stabilization (80/ 380.2-381.6)

2.22322 The method for overcoming reification that relies upon analyzing an 'I' that exists during the process of meditative stabilization (82/ 381.6-382.3)

2.22323 When one distinguishes correctly between the 'I' that exists during the process of meditative stabilization and the 'I' that does not exist in the sight of the resulting realization, both positivism and nihilism will be avoided (83/ 382.3-383.1)

2.22324 How the reifying habit fits perfectly the etymology of "ignorance" (84/ 383.1-383.4)

2.22325 One must always speak truthfully for the reason that falsehood misleads oneself and others (85/ 383.4-6)

2.232 (87/ 384.1) (86/ 383.6-384.1)

3. Concluding Remarks (86)

3.1 The Panchen Lama's humble request for patience in forgiving mistakes made while composing the text (86/ 383.6-384.1)

3.2 Signature (87/ 384.1-3)

---

[1] The commentary's page numbers are followed by the page and line numbers of the root text.

Appendix Two:

On Translating *bDag* and *bDag 'Dzin:* the hermeneutics of translating Tibetan

No translation can be truly complete. Typically, my friends who translate texts will present their handiwork to me along with some sort of apology for not getting everything perfectly right. There is no need for such apologies since those apologies imply that it is possible to get matters perfectly right. Words are not like cargo that one unloads from one boat to another; rather, their semiotic being leaves the best readers, translators, and authors ever searching for what more the words can be made to mean. Moreover, trying to tame an original author's language by means of a facile praxis of rendering equivalencies can result in submerging the text beneath an imposed methodology of translation; in fact, any praxis of translating can grow so routine that the translator may be unaware that s/he has imposed anything at all.

A good translation is one that can locate equivalences that are not limited to the identities of meaning of the separate words or fastened too exclusively to what each word bears inside it by itself. Most of the resources of a text are provided by how words derive their sense from their relations with the other words, whose semantic fields impinge upon them. Even in language, identities are not inherent, and there are interconnectedly dependent relations there too. Paying too close attention to cultivating a "literal" translation can cause one to lose sight of the forest for the trees. For this reason, a translator must take some license in selecting among polyvalent semantic possibilities, and always in the interest of communication; however, the reduction of meaning that translation necessarily entails usually causes a translator to feel some guilt; hence the apologies.

The French artist Eugene Delacroix once said that artists who seek perfection in everything are those who cannot attain it in anything. The work of translation is something like sculpting a block of stone, in that the fine work of perfecting matters has no end to it, and the more deeply that one addresses the fine details, one at a time, the more one may risk losing the communication of the presentation as a whole. That "whole" can and should dictate, and even transform, the lexical selection. At a "Training Camp on Buddhist Translation Methodology" held by Tibet House, New Delhi, in 1997,[1] there was a recommendation that translators respond to "the need for flexibility in the translation of technical terms, such as *chos*, that have more than one meaning which cannot all be conveyed by any one English term."

Refining the semantic contours of words has no endpoint: one can always find further details in synonyms that can be exploited and additional semantic threads that can be pulled. The syntactical relations that each and every change engenders may be used to more closely approach the ideal of the original text. But the original text is not a fixed asymptote, since this ideal is necessarily one's own notion. One's word-sculpture is also subject to the indignities of readers' interpretations that can provide surprising readings that were never anticipated by the translator. Despite these many difficulties, at some point it is necessary to terminate the process. The decade or more that it has taken to complete this translation should have provided enough time for considering most of the hermeneutic options.

Walter Benjamin (1997: 155) is the most articulate among those who pointed out that literal translation is impossible: "No translation would be possible if, in accord with its ultimate essence, it were to strive for similarity to the original." In spite of this insurmountable fact, humans have persisted in attempting such translations. Ultimately, there is only one language, that of human speech, or what Benjamin (1997: 156, 162) calls "pure language," and this is probably what beckons most; however, the social, linguistic, and cultural patterning of human tribes renders the life-worlds to which their speech keeps referring finite provinces of meaning. On those rare occasions when one is able to penetrate the barriers of those provinces, one finds mostly only what one is already prepared to recognize; and what is most original in a culture can remain unseen, even impenetrable. In this way, most translations say more about the translator than they do about the source society. I do not imagine that it can be very different here.

A translator who succeeds in becoming familiar with the strange may feel compelled to select ways of speaking that not only transmit lexical equivalences but also convey what is most original in the source culture, what Karl Mannheim (1952) called the *Weltanschauung*. The risk is always that word selections that are faithful to the source culture may not mean very much for the readers from the target culture; and the stranger that those lexical choices are, the greater is the chance that they will be read idiosyncratically, leaving readers lost inside of their own fabricated meanings, myopias that function like self-fulfilling prophesies. Sometimes a translator is barely able to discern what he or she has created, since the threads of the lexical choices one has made frequently lead to places that were unanticipated. Still, the translator faces a fundamental obligation to attempt to retain what is most provocative in the source exegesis, and to make that available for the readers' thoughtful consideration.

An encyclopedia could be composed with all of the terms from Tibetan Buddhism that have been only partly translated, badly translated, reformulated, experimented with and discarded, hopelessly mistranslated, et cetera, along with the many failed efforts to remedy these shortcomings. We have probably reached an era in which we have given up the idea of perfection and have learned how to accommodate ourselves to translations that succeed only partly, that communicate some aspects of an idea well while ignoring other components that the idea also includes. But that does not relieve us of the responsibility for trying to identify the shortcomings of our own attempts or to keep trying to improve our translations. One strategy for handling the dilemma of any polysemy that is unable to be carried adequately by the host language is to occasionally translate the same term in *different* ways, depending upon the context. In that way a reader will eventually be exposed to the range of meanings of a term, and word selection that is inappropriate for some circumstances can be avoided. But the reader may not know (except by footnote) that in the original text it is always the same term; further, this strategy faces the strong opposition of conservative translators, including most Tibetans, who usually adhere to a policy of translating the same word in the same way, regardless of the context.

An advantage of a policy of strict literal consistency is that a reader who is familiar with the source language can quickly learn the lexical system of a translator and recognize which are the original terms at work; however, since most readers read a translation because they do not know the source language, this benefit does not extend very far. Moreover, it can sometimes produce accounts that lack any sense at all, for by being relatively insensitive to context, it may become impossible to retrieve the context! The philosopher John Sallis (1986: 168) has observed, "Nothing could be more superficial than to sort out everything on the basis of such word-meanings." The practice may carry with it the ready comfort of certainty and order, but the true rigor of translating sometimes demands that one sustain indeterminacies, keeping them alive for further semiosis. A problem with some literalist strategies is that the confidence provided by a false sense of certainty can lull a reader into thinking that something meaningful has been conveyed, when in fact the reader (and on occasion the translator) may not have understood very much. For example, the use of "thatness" or "suchness" (*de nyid, de zhin nyid*) is so ubiquitous that readers have a ready familiarity with them without necessarily understanding them well. In order to understand the meaning of what one has translated, one needs to always assess adequacy *from the perspective of the horizon of meaning for the reader* who is construing sense from what is being read. And here it is essential to recognize that a reader reads a chapter, a text, and a culture as well as words.

The practice of literal translation wins further reinforcement from the strategy that Tibetans themselves employed when they translated Sanskrit into Tibetan. Although they too had their contestations and reformulations, for the most part they settled upon a fairly strict word-for-word, Sanskrit-to-Tibetan praxis of translation, and perhaps this has even lent greater authenticity to the Tibetan translations. But that still did not prevent the Tibetans from employing those terms differently in the context of their own religious practice.

For instance, the Tibetans translate *prajna* as *shes rab*, and they translate *jnana* sometimes as *ye shes* and other times as *shes pa*. English translators usually have translated both *shes rab* and *yeshe* as "wisdom," which leaves the English reader beginning the race already playing catch-up. One result of what the Tibetans have done is that the semiotic contrasts that are evoked in Sanskrit between *prajna* and *jnana* are not equivalent to those at work between *shes rab* and *ye shes*, since in

Sanskrit *jnana* retains the possibility of referring to any sort of mental competence or knowledge in a field of experience or inquiry and so includes both the mundane and the profound, whereas *prajna* is almost always something special and frequently implies that one has learned how to tame one's mind in areas that are related to spiritual development. Although special, *shes rab* in Tibetan is usually more mundane than is *ye she*, since the latter is frequently used to refer to that inborn awareness that a being has possessed naturally since time immemorial, and so it has a more esoteric and tantric significance. Since the more exoteric uses of *jnana* have been allocated to *shes pa*, the two Sanskrit terms have received a quasi-reversal in valuation en route to the Tibetan. Also, in the way that the Tibetans use it, it is possible that some indigenous notions of Tibetan esoteric culture have been retained in the term *ye shes.* Of course, words are always transformed by their contexts, overwhelmed by them in fact; and if modern linguistic and semiotic inquiry is to be accepted, *no word* ever is just what it is. But that is only one more argument against invoking the myth of perpetual lexical equivalences.

The Buddha himself placed priority upon effectively communicating with an audience, for the reason that there is no benefit to satisfying perfectly all of the rules that can guide correct communication if the rule-governed practice makes it impossible for people to understand what is being communicated. The most important work of translating probably takes place at a deeper, cultural level of communicating, over the length of a text, what is the form of life that has given rise to any text. The more that the reader understands the social milieu that underlies a text, the better sense the reader will be able to make of the lexical choices that are provided. So, the strategies of a translator are far more strategic than they are something strictly lexical.

Despite this situation, and the many arguments for flexibility in translation, I am compelled to defend my resolution of one lexical matter that has troubled me for decades, and that is how one best translates into English the Tibetan notion of *bdag.* I do not have much invested personally in any of the ways I have chosen to translate it; our historical task is more collaborative than that. Now that Buddhist translations from Tibetan to English have reached some maturity, it is time that we get some things more right than we have been getting them. The term *bdag* is key to Buddhism and to Tibetan philosophical culture, and its translation is only apparently simple. As most students of Tibetan Buddhism know, *bdag* means "self" as does the Sanskrit *ātma* to which it is tied. But its straightforwardness ends there because it also refers to the practice of reifying notions that function at the heart of the ignorance that it is the task of Buddhist philosophical and spiritual discipline to remove. And for that, "self" by itself simply does not cut it, especially within the Mahayana traditions of philosophical speculation.

One of the first problems that a non-Tibetan reader who encounters this word faces is the way this term *bdag* is applied both to people and to things, and so we have the peculiar coinages in English of "self of persons" and "self of phenomena." While most are able to recognize the sense of a self of persons, it strikes some readers as redundant, until they are confronted with the term "self of phenomena," which at first seems to be an idiotic phrase. Of course, confronting the idiotic can be a splendid indication that one is not reading closely enough, and so the experience can be conducive to one becoming more attentive to what a translation is doing, to the need to keep alert for what is different from what we have been accustomed to understanding, and above all to the need to reground our thinking upon an Other's life-world. Accordingly, being confronted with the idiotic can itself be salutary, and it is even inevitable if we are taking a translation seriously. The pressing problem here, however, is that we only have the phrase itself to interrogate, and an interrogation of the term "self of phenomena" will not provide us much help. Which phenomena? Are they things that are related to the self or do they also include things that are unrelated to the self? And what can "self" itself be meaning now, if it is meant to refer to things that are unrelated to the self? Here a vicious circularity appears, whereby the term is applied to make sense of a context while that context—so understood—is being applied to nail down the sense of the term.

The phrase "self of phenomena" might become more reasonable when we begin to observe that the Tibetans frequently apply the term to "the five constituents" (*pung po lnga*) that belong to a person, and a number of their discussions of "self of phenomena" concern one of these constituents. Here I will overlook the additional problem of what on earth any lay reader of English may make (if anything at all) of the phrase "the five constituents" or "the five aggregates," which has been read non-sensically for decades by many thousands of readers, and has been re-iterated by one translator after another, like a bad habit. A few translators attempt to make the phrase *pung po lnga* more readily meaningful by saying something like the five "constituents of personality" (Mabbett 2006: 32) or "the five physical, mental and emotional components of self identity" (my translation); however, nothing short of a separate essay will convey to the reader just what a "constituent" or an "aggregate" could be.[2] Simply because a hundred translators have used the term "aggregate" does not provide sufficient warrant for using a term that will not mean anything to anyone.

But my point here lies in a different direction—all of the five physical, mental and emotional components of self, while not a self of person, are at least related to a person, and so the use of the term "self" has some sense here. Similarly, the application of "self of phenomena" to objects that are possessions of a person, like the mineness of "my" hand or even "my" watch, seems reasonable. But the same practice of reifying the object of one's thinking (*dmigs yul*) can be applied to objects that are not directly related to the self, and they too are "self of phenomena."

This renders the use of "self" to translate *bdag* inadequate. For this reason, English translators have employed another term, "entity," which captures the broader range of application of *bdag*. As usual in translation, what is gained in one respect can be lost in another, since the preponderance of occasions in which *bdag*, and even *chos kyi bdag* ("self of phenomena"), is used does have reference to an actual human self, and one is reluctant to lose this common association. "Entity," however, at least has the benefit of capturing the full epistemological scope of the matters that are being scrutinized by Mahayana scholarship. But here yet another caution is needed: Mahayana scholars are not doing only epistemology, and any analysis that remains strictly epistemological runs the risk of escaping the Buddhist *Weltanschauung*, and even distorting it. For Mahayana scholars, their careful, rational epistemological inquiries were always accompanied by some soteriological or "spiritual" attention to the practical aspects of actually cultivating a mind that acts habitually on the basis of wisdom, an interest "to which ultimately rational analysis was only an accessory" (Mabbett 2006: 23).

This is not to say that these thinkers, from Nāgārjuna to Gendun Chophel, were not as formal analytical as they could possibly be, and even Tibetans complain that Tibetan formal analysis can be excessively rational. At several points in this text the Panchen Lama himself satirizes practitioners who are exclusively focused upon the formal analytical. Nevertheless, it must be accepted that the primary interest of Mahayana scholars has been to effect enduring changes to the ways that one acts and thinks; quite subtly, these scholars recognize that such changes are not simple matters of logic but require a thorough and usually gradual *practice* of reprogramming one's habits of behavior. As Western philosophers we are perhaps too ready to distort Buddhist thought in the direction of epistemology. By doing so we may make too little of the way that Tibetans always think in terms of the broader mental continuum that will persist in guiding our actions after our deliberative investigations have ceased, a continuum that mostly runs by itself as a consequence of the habits (sometimes called karma) of routine conceptualization that a person has developed. This insight motivates not only scholarly reflection in Tibet but the orientation of Tibetan lay people as well, including those who are not literate, so this orientation is very widespread.

This idea is already invested in the notion of *sgom*, although this aspect sometimes gets overlooked when *sgom* is translated as "meditation." In fact, *sgom* means "cultivation," "habituation," or "familiarization" more than it means sitting cross-legged on the floor in some kind of mentally induced era of good feelings. The practice of *sgom* involves making something second nature: it is a practice that permits practitioners a way to integrate a valued insight into one's psychophysical comportment in a manner that causes it to endure. What the Tibetans are describing is that the solution to a human problem like suffering does not center as much upon having a realization as it does upon making that realization habitually operative within one's natural ways of acting and abiding in the everyday world. Perhaps millions of people have been misled, at least in part, by the way that we keep translating *sgom*, narrowing and obfuscating its scope. Similarly, while philosophical analysis and reflection are involved, the real focus of attention is a practice of gradually transforming the habitual patterns of one's mundane activities. That is why the Gelug founder Tsong Khapa put the *rim* ("gradual," "progressive," "by stages") in Atisha's *lam* ("path"), and this may be the centermost insight of Tibetan philosophical culture.

Many of my colleagues in Western philosophy, including those in phenomenology, regularly exclude any of the Indian or Chinese systems of formal epistemological reflection from the domain of "philosophy." They argue variously that it is not value-free and open-ended, and generally involves having an accepted religious framework. In return I point out to them that European philosophy has never been truly value free or open-ended either—even dialectics for Hegel had its *telos*—and that Western philosophy developed in close association with the scholastic traditions of European Christianity. One colleague replied to my concern this way, "Let me boil it down to one simple fact—philosophy originated in Greece, and anything that does not trace its origin back to Greece cannot be philosophy." I once shared this myopic perspective over lunch with Prof. R. S. Tripathi, the renowned Buddhist scholar from Varanasi, India. He said to me, "They are right. What Buddhism does is not philosophy! Philosophy wishes never to concern itself with helping people evolve in practical ways, and it strives always to remain remote and abstract. In India, we have little interest in such a perspective."

The beatnik poet Charles Olsen once said that in America it's not what you know that counts, but what you can do with what you know, and the Mahayana scholars take a similar perspective. To turn Buddhist scholars into value-free philosophers who have a strictly professional interest in the truth and do not have an equal concern for what could be the practical consequences of their inquiries[3] is to make a hash of Buddhist thinking.

For this reason we need to conceive of the problem of *bdag* and its associated *bdag 'dzin* in a manner that retains the Buddhist process-oriented investigations of the phenomenon. *Bdag 'dzin* is the habitual practice of fixating upon each entity as having an inherent essence of its own, independently of other entities. It is frequently translated (refer to any dictionary) as "self-grasping," but that translation is a myopic literalism that fails to adequately appreciate the Tibetan thinking. Just how does "self-grasping" capture or convey the profound idea of "the habitual practice of fixating upon each entity as having an inherent essence of its own, independently of other entities"? First, "self-grasping" is too static a notion. *Bdag 'dzin* is an ongoing *praxis* of thinking and acting: it is more a verb than a noun. Included within *'dzin* are the notions of "apprehending," "perceiving," and "seizing" *in ways that are habitual*. While "grasping" is one of its aspects, it is a practice that is much more pervasive than those occasional occurrences when we overly fixate upon a notion in a compulsive way: it is not a special occasion but the *normal* way that people naturally think and perceive most of the time. *Bdag 'dzin*, then, is more than "self-grasping," and it means the habitual apprehending of entities as things that exist inherently in-themselves in just the way we have conceived them. Well that is a mouthful; moreover, it excludes the most frequent instantiation of *dag 'dzin*, which is the reification of a personal self.

Throughout translating this text by the great Panchen Lama Lobsang Chökyi Gyaltsen, which bears the short title, *Bdag 'dzin gshags 'debs*, I struggled over how to translate *bdag 'dzin.* I wanted to avoid "self-grasping" because that fails to capture the epistemological scope of the problem. It had the further difficulty that since the Panchen Lama's text is a spirited philosophical-cum-spiritual debate between *bdag 'dzin* and *she rab* (wisdom), using "self-grasping" had the unwelcome consequence of immediately placing any reader against anything so terrible sounding state of affairs as "self-grasping" *before* any of the argumentation was considered, removing from the book much of its dramatic tension. In the text, the debate commences with *bdag 'dzin* gaining the upper-hand, and the tension produced by this is essential to the text's success. More a philosophical comedy than is *Faust*, the convincing arguments made by *bdag 'dzin* are what engage the reader's interest, and as a narrative strategy I especially wanted to use this tension to hook the reader into paying closer attention than is usual to the detailed philosophical defense by wisdom in Chapters 5 and 7 of the text. Even more than that, *bdag 'dzin* does not only refer to the reification of the self, it involves how we go about thinking erroneously about every notion that we entertain. It is important that the very broad scope of that practice, exercised by most persons including most readers, be retained.

For a time I translated *bdag 'dzin* as "the habit of reifying entities, including the self," which was my futile effort to capture the best of both worlds. This quickly became unwieldy, since the term reoccurs too frequently, including several occasions when *bdag 'dzin* begins a new turn of speaking; after only a few pages, the phrase became tedious even to me, and I was forced to discard it. Even simply "the habit of reifying entities" was too awkward for continuous use, and while pertinent, the conceptual aspect it conveys does not include all of the psychological aspects of practice and karma that are involved. I used "reification" itself for a time, but I was concerned about the possible unfamiliarity of the term to many non-philosophical readers. So, I was led back to "self-grasping," which at least had the benefit that fewer people objected to it. Further, it is an accurate rendition of the original Sanskrit *ātmagraha* to which it is tied, which principally is "self-grasping."[4] But does it successfully convey what is needed? Because this text is an original Tibetan composition, I felt less obligated to retain strict ties to Sanskrit equivalences. Amidst all of these uncertainties, I began to feel that I was failing as a translator.

I am not alone with my indecisiveness about translating *bdag*. Sera Me Khensur Lobsang Tharchin, whose commentary on *Bdag 'dzin gshags 'debs* I consulted after my first draft of the translation had been completed (which was based upon the commentary of Sera Je Khensur Lobsang Tsering), expresses similar frustration with finding an adequate English equivalent for *bdag 'dzin*. At this point Khensur Lobsang Tharchin even jests that his life would be made much simpler if he had not learned any English at all. Khensur Rinpoche questioned his American students in New Jersey:

> Are *bdag 'dzin* and 'egotism,' or 'egoism,' the same? *Bdag 'dzin* is the opposite of *stong nyid* [emptiness]. 'Ego' cannot be *bdag* because egotism cannot be the opposite of *stong nyid*. If we can't use 'egotism,' then can we use 'ignorance' for translating *bdag 'dzin*? In the way Tibetans use ignorance, there are many kinds of ignorance, so ignorance is not necessarily *bdag 'dzin*. For example, there is an ignorance about impermanence that would not be *bdag 'dzin*. Similarly, ignorance about karma would not be *bdag 'dzin*. So, what is the best way to translate *bdag 'dzin*? It is very difficult for me.

The translators for Choden Rinpoche during his commentary on *Bdag 'dzin gshags 'debs* in California always used "ignorance" for *bdag 'dzin*, without giving any indication that it had any problematic features. Because of this, the serious students that were there were left in the dark, put at some disadvantage in their efforts to grasp the fundamental import of the text. I did not wish to repeat such an error for my readers; however, using an eight-word phrase such as I just described is also not a reasonable solution. At one point Michael Roach correctly suggested to Khensur Lobsang Tharchin, "I don't think there is a single word that will translate *bdag 'dzin*. English words do not automatically have Buddhist meanings. So if you want to use English words, you have to explain."

Then I came upon a possible solution—that the mundane practice of reifying entities that *bdag 'dzin* refers to is the sort of everyday positivism that people employ when they use common sense. The term "common sense" refers to people who act upon the immanent concerns that face them, without any formal analysis or philosophical scrutiny being applied. The term has both positive and negative connotations, and so if I used that to render *bdag 'dzin*, the reader might be inclined to take the arguments of *bdag 'dzin* more seriously. The term's positive connotations come from the way that when thinking is formalized it quickly becomes trapped inside the fixed notions it has set up for itself, and common sense can sometimes find ways to ignore those traps. But wisdom in the sense of *shes rab* is learning how to continuously remove the concretized notions that any practice of formal thinking produces and how to remain open to the possibilities for further evolution. From this perspective the negative aspects of common sense—its narrow-mindedness, its self-congratulatory nature (which always seems to be a component of ignorance), and its concern for gaining material benefits—can be highlighted. Best of all, "common sense" captures *a practice* of reflection that is self-perpetuating and bears associations that are psychological as well as epistemological, so it comes fairly close to reflecting the scope of Mahayana analysis. As Benjamin (1997: 159) has said, sometimes the most that a translation can achieve is "an echo of the original" in which there occurs some "reverberation" of the idea in the source language. I thought that "common sense" echoes the dynamism and self-propelling quality of the ignorance of *bdag 'dzin*, and might lead readers to interrogate more critically their own mundane practices of thinking.

So, for a time I went with common sense, and the short title of my translation became "The Debate Between Wisdom and Common Sense." But I kept having second-thoughts; however, it is not so easy to find another term as multi-dimensional as "common sense" or that captures equally the epistemological features in the appropriate context.

There is additional support for my broader interpretation of *bdag 'dzin* in the Panchen Lama's text by his own practice of alternating the name that he gives to the opponent of wisdom. Throughout the text, *bdag 'dzin* and *bden 'dzin*, are used interchangeably. *Bden 'dzin* means the habit of thinking that entities have true, inherent existence, and it can also be translated by the phrase "truth habits" or on occasion even "truth-grasping." What is intended is a practice of thinking in which one reifies each notion one thinks as it arises. If Panchen Lobsang Chökyi Gyaltsen really meant only "self"-grasping, he would not have alternated it with "truth"-grasping, which has a much more epistemological reference. Instead, when he uses either term he is referring to our *everyday practice of reificatory thinking.*

Further, in the last year I went carefully through a commentary to the Panchen Lama's text that was written a century and a half ago by a Shigatse lama named Lobsang Jinpa.[5] After the introductory praises and initial statement of the objective of the text and before the commentary on the debate between wisdom and common sense commences blow-by-blow, Lobsang Jinpa offers what he calls "a transitional comment" (*'tshams sbyar*), during which he explains concisely that it is the purpose of the text to refute the object produced by the mode of apprehending of *bdag 'dzin* (*bdag 'dzin gyi 'dzin stang kyi yul sun phyung*) and to realize the emptiness of any entity that has instinctively become objectified in and as *bdag 'dzin*'s habitual practice of concretizing it (*bdag 'dzin lhan skyes kyi dmigs par gyur pa'i bdag de'i bdag med*). From this it becomes evident that the target of the Panchen Lama's text is the mundane practice of thinking that most people share. Self-grasping is one of the results of that praxis of thinking, but the practice itself exceeds being addressed exclusively to a personal self. While the latter must be included, it should not be to the exclusion of everything else. Lobsang Jinpa's frequent use of the phrase "objects reified by *bdag 'dzin*'s way of apprehending" reinforces my belief that *bdag 'dzin* has to be translated by a term that is very broad in its epistemological scope.

During some conversations with colleagues about this question, I came upon another salutary phrase, "customary identification," as a way to capture how *bdag 'dzin* functions in this text, which affords the apt opportunity of using the parallel term "identity" for *bdag*. This solution lacks the poetic reach of "common sense," which accommodates well the dramatic personalization that the concept *bdag 'dzin* / *bden 'dzin* receives at the hands of the Panchen Lama; but "customary identification" avoids many of the flaws of the other alternatives, which made it compelling for a time. In the end, however, I concluded that its proximity to "conventional truth" would produce unhelpful confusion.

I again reconsidered "reification," which has the advantage of being both correct and particularly apt.

Moreover, "reification" opposes well its antagonist "wisdom," as the two are practically antonyms in the way that Tibetans use them (and being antonyms was the criterion that Khensur Lobsang Tharchin wanted to apply). But its problem is that many readers may be unfamiliar with it, and some readers have become so familiar with the pertinence of *bdag 'dzin / bden 'dzin* to egoism that its absence might make them even less inclined to tolerate "reification," even though it is the main point of the term. In the end, I returned to using a slightly longer version of "reification" that has the attribute of being perfectly accurate. So we find ourselves with "the reifying habit." Yes: that is *bdag 'dzin / bden 'dzin.*

One could say that absolutism, in all of its guises, is the Panchen Lama's target, as is the case with much Mahayana analysis. Other texts, including some Gelug texts but especially texts from the other three Tibetan sects, emphasize the need to refute *mtshan ma*, which is another hard nugget for English translators. Having the meaning "sign" or "mark" (many readers are unsure about just what they are supposed to do with "mark"), it usually refers to the proliferation of notions each of which is wrongly considered to have independent being. While *mtshan ma* can be used to refer to any idea or judgment regardless of its merit, it is frequently used when some absolutist sense is entertained and when one holds that what lacks inherent existence has such inherent existence. I would describe *mtshan ma* as a feature of thinking that is the means by which the unity of identification that one has developed is projected upon a thing and afterward reified as the thing's essential nature.

Explained in semiotic terms, *mtshan ma* is a sign to which a specific significance has been allocated, that is, a signified that has been fixed inside of a particular signifier. The problem is that the project of fixing the meaning of signs is interminable, since signs are never themselves but are only what they come to refer to, a process that Saussure (1959) has insisted is purely arbitrary. If Saussure is right, then the strategy of settling upon one correct meaning or equivalent term for each word is mistaken and doomed to failure, and any word is perpetually vulnerable to semantic transformation by the other words that accompany it.[6] Moreover, it strikes me that this semiotic position is highly compatible with Madhyamaka thinking, for which the context plays a vital role in the process of mutual determination by which a phenomenon gains its sense and reference. This helps explain the inevitable situation that "fidelity in translating the individual word can almost never fully render the meaning it has in the original" (Benjamin 1997: 160).

The objective of a translator should always include an attempt to convey accurately some comprehensive glimpses of the worldly context in which the original author was operating, for it is the life-world of the original author that informs the reader of a translation about how to understand the words the author and translator are using. The more remote that the culture of the original language of a translated text is to the culture of the host language, the more important it is to translate carefully not only on the lexical level, but to pay some attention to conveying the sociocultural dimensions of the text to the reader, at least to the extent that the aesthetic aims of the text can tolerate. In the end, my conclusion was that "the reifying habit" is the most informative translation for *bdag 'dzin / bden 'dzin*, and the most proximate to the intention of the Panchen Lama.

---

[1] Alexander Berzin (1997: 2).

[2] For a decent and concise explanation of "the five aggregates" see Verdu 1981: 6-8.

[3] Being "professional" sometimes require that one refuse to be invested personally in the practical consequences of one's investigations.

[4] This raises the interesting philological question of whether the meaning of the term may have been transformed by the way that Tibetans have adopted it.

[5] Lobsang Jinpa (*bLo bzang sbyin pa*), *Relinquishing the Extreme Views Belonging to Reification: An Explanation of the Meaning of the Great Mudra's Basis, Path, and Result* (*gZhi lam 'bras bu'i phyag chen gyi don rnam par dshad 'dzin mthar skrod*).

[6] For a detailed account of this phenomenon see Liberman 2012.

Bibliography

Anonymous. nd. *Dpal gsang ba 'dus pa'i blo brgud gsol 'debs dang bdag bskyed ngag 'don bkra shis lhun po rgyud pa grva tsang (The Tashi Lhunpo Tantric College's daily recitation of reverence for the lineage of masters and self-generation as the sublîme Lord of the Secret)*, Dharamsala, India: Tibetan Cultural Printing Press.

Benjamin, Walter. 1997. "The Translator's Task" of the Translator." Trans. by Steven Rendall. *TTR : traduction, terminologie, rédaction*, vol. 10, no. 2, p. 151-165. Also in *Illuminations: Essays and Reflections.* Ed., with an introduction, by Hannah Arendt. Trans. by Harry Zohn. New York: Harcourt, Brace & World. Pp. 69-82.

Berger, Peter. 1963. *An Invitation to Sociology.* New York: Doubleday.

Berger, Peter and Thomas Luckmann. 1966. *The Social Construction of Reality: an essay in the sociology of knowledge.* New York: Doubleday.

Berzin, Alexander. 1997. "Training Camp on Buddhist Translation Methodology." *Tibet House Bulletin*, Vol. 12, No. 2, pp. 1-5.

Duff, Tony. 2009. *The Illuminator Tibetan-English Encyclopedic Dictionary.* Kathmandu, Nepal: Padma Karpo Translation Committee.

Garfinkel, Harold. 2002. *Ethnomethodology's Program.* Lanham, MD: Rowman & Littlefield.

Gorampa Sonam Senge (*go ram pa bsod nams seng gel* 1428-1489). nd. *lta ba'i shen 'byed* (*Distinguishing the Views*). Sarnath, India: Sakya Sutdents' Union.

Hegel, G.W.F. 1969. *Hegel's Science of Logic*. Atlantic Highlands, NJ: Humanities Press.

Hopkins, Jeffrey. 1992. *Tibetan-Sanskrit-English Dictionary.* Charlottesville, VA: University of Virginia Tibetan Studies Program.

Jackson, Roger R. 2006. "Deconstruction and Foundationalist Tendencies in Indian and Tibetan Buddhism." In Jin Y. Park (ed), *Buddhisms and Deconstructions*. Lanham, Maryland: Rowman & Littlefield.

Liberman, Kenneth. 2004. *Dialectical Practice in Tibetan Philosophical Culture*. Lanham, MD: Rowman & Littlefield.

_________. 2012. "Semantic Drift in Conversations." *Human Studies* 35 (2). Pp. 263-277. (DOI) 10.1007/s10746-012-9225-1.

_________. 2013. *More Studies in Ethnomethodology*. Albany, NY: SUNY Press.

Lobsang Jinpa. nd. (*blo bzang spyiṇ pa*; circa 1850). *Relinquishing the Extreme Views Belonging to Reification: An Explanation of the Meaning of the Great Mudra's Basis, Path, and Result* (*gzhi lam 'bras bu'i phyag chen gyi don rnam par dshad pa bdag 'dzin mthar scrod*). Shigatse: Ganden Choling Hermitage.

Longchenpa (*kLong chen rab 'byams*; 1308-1364). 2001. *The Precious Treasury of the Basic Space of Phenomena* (*chos *dbyins rin po che'i mdzod*). Junction City, CA: Padma Publishing.

Mabbett, Ian. 2006. "Nāgārjuna and Deconstruction." In Jin Y. Park (ed), *Buddhisms and Deconstructions*. Lanham, Maryland: Rowman & Littlefield.

Mannheim, Karl. 1952. "On the Interpretation of *Weltanschauung*." In *Essays on the Sociology of Knowledge*. London: Routledge.

Nāgārjuna. 2009. *Ratnāvalī of Ācārya Nāgārjuna with the Commentary by Ajitamitra* (Tib. *Rin chen phreng ba*). Ngawang Samten (ed). Sarnath, India: Central Institute of Higher Tibetan Studies.

Olsen, Charles. 1983. *The Maximus Poems*. Berkeley, Calif.: University of California Press.

Rigzin, Tsepak. 1986. *Tibetan-English Dictionary of Buddhist Terminology*. Dharamsala: Library of Tibetan Works and Archives

Sallis, John. 1986. *Delimitations*. Bloomington, Indiana: Indiana University Press.

_________. 2002. *On Translation*. Bloomington, Indiana: Indiana University Press.

Saussure, Ferdinand de. 1959. *Course in General Linguistics*. New York: Philosophical Library.

Smith, E. Gene. 2001. *Among Tibetan Texts*. Boston: Wisdom Publications.

Verdu, Alfonso. 1981. *The Philosophy of Buddhism*. The Hague: Martinus Nijhoff.

Index